Watford P

a
Pictorial History

J B Nunn

Contributors
Edgar Chapman BA *(early history)*
George Lorimer *(contemporary history)*
Linda V Nunn *(colour advisor)*

Contents

Photographic Credits
Barry Anthony: 86t, 96, 100t, 101b, **David Spain Archives:** 50t & b, 125t
Heale Bequest, Camden PL: 14, 15; **Harry Williamson:** 72; **Author/F Stafford Dupree:** 4 & 5t
Private Collection: 22t, 25b, 34t, 36b, 37t, 49t, 58t, 86c b, 96b, 106, 107b; **Andy Sands:** 9, 43t
Watford Library Collection: 6 to 9t, 10, 11 Britton, 12, 13, 16, 17, 20, 21t, 22b, 26, 27t, 28, 30, 33t, 34b,
36t, 39b, 40, 41, 43b, 44t, 45t, 49b, 51, 52, 57, 58b, 59t, 60, 65, 99b
WL/George Bolton: 31b, 54, 59b, 63; **WL/William Coles:** 23t, 24, 31t, 32, 35b, 38, 41, 46b
WL/John Cullen 10   **WL/Cardiff Aero Services:** 57   **WL /Frederick Downer:** 17, 23b, 25
WL/Greville Collection: 66, 67, 68, 69, 70, 71   **WL/F H Haines:** 29, 35t, 42, 53, 56
WL/Tempest: 88, 90; **WL/Whitford Anderson:** 27b; 39t;
WL/Watford Illustrated/Downer: 23b, 47, 48
WL/Wat Obs: 65   **WM:** 19, 45b, 62   **WM/Greville Studios:** 87b
Wat Obs/A Gregory: 100b, 101t   **West Herts Post:** 20 (top, old Buck inset)
Wat Obs, Harry Williamson: 82, 83, 84, 98
Author: 64, 73-75, 76-78, 79-81, 85, 87t, 91-93, 94, 95, 97, 99t, 102-105, 107-109,
110-112, 113-115, 116-118, 119-120, 121-124, 125c b, 128 and comparison insets.
Most of the early photographs are from the Watford Central Library's Local Collection and the
photographers indicated above, where known.

WL=Watford Central Library: **WM**=Watford Museum.

Foreword

When this work was published in 1999 it filled a niche for those who wanted a small guide to Watford's history with text and captions explaining facts and details beyond the images. With this reprint the opportunity has been taken to undertake a small amount of up-dating to reflect local changes with added pictures of the past few years .

Each and every illustration represents a landmark of one sort or another and, with the exception of the few modern pictures, each represents an era or way of life that has disappeared. Those who remember an early journey by bus up Scots Hill—and of having to get out and walk while the bus struggled up the 1 in 8 gradient—are now few and far between. But many youngsters and newcomers, having been told tales of the past, find difficulty in relating modern times to 50 or more years ago. It is very difficult to identify old places and long gone landmarks. Rebuilding is so quick that it is only from such a book as this that those who wish can get a better idea of how and where our forebears lived. To help solve some of the queries a number of illustrations have 'modern' pictures as inserts.

That a picture is in colour adds to the realism as, notwithstanding the charm of 'black and white', there is in that medium a vital dimension missing. It is salutary to remember that the early photographs were taken with cumbersome cameras for which the photographer had to prepare his plates; and that many glass plates still survive. By the early 1920's plates and roll film vied in popularity among skilled workers – and roll film, and 'Brownie cameras', held sway until in the mid-1950's the demand for colour had to satisfied. This was with colour transparencies and slide projection until colour print film became commonplace.

Now, film cameras are in danger of becoming objects of the past as 'digital' is sweeping all before. There are in this book photographs from all processes, as well as computer assisted colouring of the very many earlier black and white photos.

Dates as 'c19**' or 'about c19**' are as close as research permits. Dates that are unqualified are reasonably certain. The photographs are derived from the 'Book of Watford 2nd Edition', and from 'Watford Past'.

The 'Book of Watford, 2nd Edition' is available for those who wish to explore in greater depth Watford's history.

J B (Bob) Nunn

Introduction

It is a standing joke that, in Watford, if there is an old building remaining it must be one that the Council has missed. There is, of course, a good deal of truth in the saying. The funny thing is that whilst people admire the new buildings, after a short while they hanker after recollections and memories of what was there before! It is quite understandable that many residents would not know where the 'Green Man' pub was, or the 'Rose and Crown', or that we had several cinemas in the town centre, and as many as seven altogether at one time.

Nostalgia comes into full play when pictures of the Park Gates are shown; "Where were they?" is asked. "Why were they knocked down?" is the question which follows. There is a quietness when it is realised that they came down for road widening. There is disquiet that so much space should be taken at the town hall underpass, and that the Parade is disfigured with a flyover. There is resentment that so much retail development is permitted which hugely increases car use within the town, but yet the very workers and inhabitants it has been designed to attract, are enjoined to forsake their cars. The priorities—even to a child—do not seem to make sense.

The pressure to expand, inwards, is immense; it pleases the Harlequin Centre—a sub-regional shopping centre—and the shopkeepers who have to find the high rents which please the landlords. It pushes up house prices, making everyone feel richer; the treadmill turning faster to stand still.

When time comes to stand aside for a while there is entertainment at the Town Hall's 'Colosseum'—including renowned classical concerts; the recently refurbished Watford Palace Theatre, one of the country's few live provincial theatres, regularly features top flight plays and can be relied upon for the traditional Christmas Pantomime. The Pump Theatre is a compact 'comedy and drama' and local community playhouse, and for those who like their evening entertainment rather more raw there are several clubs in the town's 'Cafe Quarter'. Spectator sport majors around famed Vicarage Road where the next few seasons will be interesting to see how Watford make out in the Premier division, and whether the Saracens can continue to hold their own. The YMCA, at Charter Place, has a restaurant, meetings rooms and regularly offers a variety of 'keep-fit and healthy-activities', but Watford has no town-centre cinemas.

Watford Museum, with the 'Watford Springs' Swimming and Leisure complex adjacent*, reflects the importance to Watford of its earlier printing and brewing industries. Watford Central Library, in a quiet precinct opposite the Town Hall, offers, in addition to normal book lending facilities, both CD and Video loan and is rightly renowned for its 'local' collection of books, maps and miscellaneous documents so essential in tracing roots and rights of modern life.

When all else fails Watford has the final means of escape; the rail line between Watford and Euston which is covered in just a little over twenty minutes giving quick access to London's stores, museums, cinemas and theatres. Watford, however, has no bus station, as such. There is a congregation of buses in the High Street, outside Woolworth's, and in Market Street; there is sometimes a lesser gathering in the Market Place opposite the Post Office. For the unwary, Watford has a one-way ring road that causes confusion to motorists new to it, and aggravation to townspeople who did not like its pedestrian underpasses. Watford's Market started with ancient rights granted centuries ago and which fell into disuse; it was held in the Market Place until 1928, and then moved off the High Street to behind the Midland Bank (HSBC). The whole area was revamped in the late 1960s as Charter Place and the popular Market is held on Tuesdays, Fridays and Saturdays in its Market Hall.

Since this intro was penned in 1999 Watford Springs fell apart and was demolished; a reputed £12,000,000 was thus wasted. The town centre has been enhanced; the shops fronting St Mary's Church pulled down and St Mary's Square created, colloquially known as the 'Patio'. Sun Printer's site is being redeveloped. W H Smith withdrew from the High Street. The Museum has been found to be under-used and a project mooted that a large 'Civic Quarter' be built near the town hall, to include theatre, new swimming complex, museum, multi-storey car park and 200 to 300 flats, etc.

A proposal to put flats upon the Clement's site fell to a new store taking over. We have a new branch of Woolworths, and new motel in Water Lane, the road closed for five months while an effort was made to control flooding!

But, as always, myriad bodies of people, quietly and largely unsung, contribute good work, care, transport and funding to those less fortunate than the majority.

The ford was not always in flood and this is an artist's impression of how the ford may have looked nearly two millennia ago on an early autumn day, c AD250. The man on foot is already in the water and, once around the bend, in the distance he has to face a steep hill. This may be a realm of fancy and you may like to see what nearly the same spot looked like in AD 1989. If so, please see page 128.

This story is that of Watford Street; for, until other roads were built off it, that was the name by which it was once known. In a Church Vestry record, 1657, listing church land, it is stated, "Two tenements adjoining together between the house of John Hart on the North and a house of John Anderson's on the South and abutting upon Watford Street on the East", and "Four tenements adjoining together standing between the house of Ralph Heywood on the South and the house of Ralph Beckford on the North and abutting upon Watford Street".

The Street has seen more shades of life than we can imagine, from pedlars and stocks in the Market Place, through corn milling and brewing. It has had its share of festivities and processions, from Weddings and Coronations to the triumphant return of the team after scoring Premiership promotion. It has had more than its fair share of derision about its length and unkempt appearance.

It was left to its own devices until growth in population led to insanitary conditions and bad health caused it to be governed by the Local Board of Health, from 1850, but it survived. It had wells dug along its length to provide water, and it has seen fires and floods.

Its markets, and then its shops, acted as a magnet drawing people from a wide radius.

The Street developed an air of insularity, of self-satisfaction even, for it had everything of importance. But left on its own it contributed little growth; it only served.

It was left to the industry which followed the railway, and the housing estates, to create the demand for goods, which the Street's shops were only too happy to satisfy. In that, the Street was 'wanted' and content. Though it had to share its wealth with Queen Street, 1860, and with Watford New Town's shops in St Albans Road between Station Road and the railway bridge, they did not give serious competition.

The early few shops — houses converted in a rudimentary manner — coped with a population of a few thousand; then gradually, houses were taken down and rebuilt as 'proper' shops. The Street's market and revamped shops continued to attract trade. Two wars came and went and the time came

An artist's impression of the ford, looking north, as in circa AD750. Henry Williams, in his 'History of Watford' wrote, in 1880, "Some years ago, when excavating at the Watford Gas Works, the workmen found a number of bones, which Dr Brett pronounced as human. The theory this introduces is that the ford across the town was much wider than the present stream and that some unfortunate man tried to cross it on horseback and both were lost in the swamp; the other bones were those of wild deer with which the woods of this county abounded centuries ago."

when the Street found that, after all, its charm had worn thin and that Hemel Hempstead and Brent Cross, especially, were breathing hard down its length and taking trade. The Street, on its own, could no longer cope and a shopping centre adjacent was conceived and built. The Harlequin Centre restored the town's eminence as a shopping town, but, in doing so, drained the lifeblood from the Street, relegating it to a 'has-been'. After a decade a slow resurgence started and the Street is taking on a different role and a new character.

It had been beaten almost into submission by being over-populated and ground down by motor vehicles, and although being the constant source of attention by local Government for fifty years, it is little improved. It is fitting that we start at the Ford, nearly two thousand years ago, and see where the tale takes us.

Right: These finely crafted bronze artifacts are some found in 1960 when foundations were being dug near Greenhill Crescent. They are a Belt Buckle, Spear Head, Bronze Bowl, Axe Head and are in Watford's Museum

Watford, from Chalk Hill, Bushey, c1813, and 2004

Was the ford the origin of Watford's naming?

The origins of Watford's name are scanty and impossible to define. That a ford was in existence was common knowledge, as was the degree of its importance. Anyone travelling from London, northwards would descend the hill and face the river. If it was in a good mood it could be waded across. If in flood it would have presented a formidable barrier, in depth, in width, and in the extent to which it would extend up- and down-stream. There were no alternative places to cross within a considerable distance.

The first Watford Bridge was built by laymen under control of St Alban's Abbey, its owners, and was almost certainly a footbridge; the river, under normal circumstances was fairly shallow and horses (and carts with their large wheels) would not be inconvenienced. The major early trackway, along which the town grew in the 12th century, was from London via Watling Street to Stanmore and then through Wat-ford to Aylesbury or Leighton Buzzard, along the Gade Valley. In the impression, p5, the bridge is shown as fairly long. In reality, to span the marshy borders, it may well have been much longer. A record of metes and bounds, in 1605, describes starting the journey at 'Townsend Bridge' or 'Great Bridge of Watford'. David Downer is more prosaic when he describes it as being in the 1850s 'a narrow one, with a ford alongside for the horses and carts'. His recollections were penned in 1916, recounted by W R Saunders, and may be considered as reliable.

Throughout much of its history we may suppose that it has been no more than a footbridge, and in time was replaced by wooden structures with the capability of accepting horse and carts; and then, later still, being brick-built. With the growth of the town (particularly after the cessation of the tolls) the bridge faced heavier wear. It was complained of in 1887 as 'with the supports blocking the passage of rotting weeds' and by Dr Brett, again, in an Annual Report on the state of the town's health in 1890, when he remarked about 'the crumbling Colne Bridge'. A satisfactory structure was built by 1895 and at last we had a bridge, and the ford, as such, was confined to history.

As far as the name is concerned opinion seems to be settling on the fact that, being likely to flood easily, the first element is 'Wæt' meaning full of water, hence Wæt-ford.

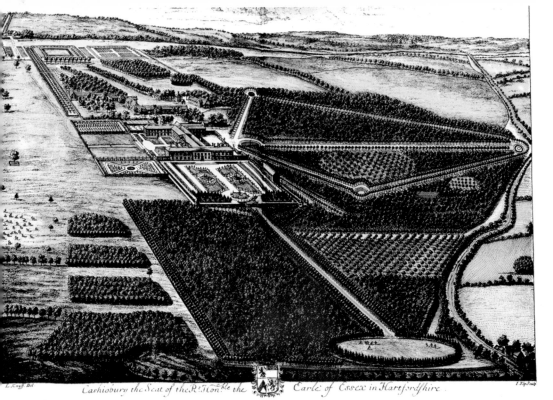

Cashiobury the Seat of the Rt Honble the Earle of Essex in Hartfordshire.

Cassiobury, c1700. The road at the right leads from Cassio Hamlet along to the Grove and thence towards Home Park (Langlebury). The House, and wooded grounds below and to its right, became Cassiobury estate. The grassy ground with four small wooded areas became our Cassiobury Park. Where the apex of paths meet at the right is about where Ridge Lane is. At the time of this Knyff & Kip drawing Algernon, 2nd Earl of Essex, was in possession.

c1900/1910; Drayton Ford, Springwell Lane, Mill End. Watford's river would have been wider and deeper but the original 'bridge' may well have been similar though longer. The river was 'widened' by the passage of horses and carts wearing down the banks as shown on both 1871 and 1896 Ordnance Survey Maps. Wooden bridges were over the Colne at Wiggenhall Rd and the Gade and canal at Croxley until mid-1920's.

Enlarged 1857 by J.B. Ross

Based on Ordnance Survey 1822

8

In the Domesday Book Bushey is rated at 'two mills' and Cashio at 'four mills' with Watford not being listed. Here, this sale notice indicates that there were, in 1838, two mills at this spot, one of which had been turned to paper-making and the other was a corn mill. Whether they had any ancestry with the mills of Domesday times is perhaps doubtful.

We may only conjecture about early mills for, with the later advent of canals, many would change function to paper making or fall into disuse. Likely sites were Grove; Cassiobury (old mill); Watford, and Hampermill.

A 'new mill' was near Swiss Cottage from c1620 to c1750. In 1770 the mediaeval Oxhey mill site was revived as Rookery Silk Mill.

Just one year after the railway opened, Bushey Mills are up for sale. Note the location on the map, left.

To be disposed of by Tender,

THE LEASE AND FIXTURES OF

Bushey Mills,

WATFORD, HERTS.

80 Years of the Lease to come from Michaelmas day next, at a low Rent, at which Time it may be entered upon, the proposals to be delivered Sealed up to MR. STEVENS, on the premises, on or before the 28th; day of July next, where Letters directed Post paid, or any 'application made, further information will be given: and no proposals will be attended to which are offered after 12 o'Clock, on the above day.

The above named Mills are exceeding advantageously and pleasantly situated, 14 Miles from London, 2 from the Navigation, and only a few Miles from several respectable Market Towns; the Mills now consists of a one Vat paper Mill, with all its gear-work, Presses, Engine, and all other requisites for making paper.

Also a Corn Mill with two pair of Stones, 4 dressing Mills, and other tackling will be included in the above disposal, both Mills are worked on the same head, and capable of great improvement, having a strong stream of water equal to drive two powerful Wheels, carrying 6 Engines or 6 pair of Stones, and at no time of the Year is short of water, and near 7 Feet fall; the whole may be converted into a Paper or Corn Mill as may be required: in addition to which there is a Beautiful spring of clear water which produces the finest colours.

A modern built House, a large Barn, Stable and sundry other out-buildings, a Pleasure ground and Kitchen garden well stocked with Fruit Trees, and upwards of Eleven Acres of meadow Land, with the right of Fishing belonging to the said Mills·

** ROUGH TIMBER FOR REPAIRS WILL BE FOUND.

The Term will be extended to 60, Years if required, the Lessee finding their own materials for building.

N.B. the parlour has got a door

Scale and Bates, Printers, 160, Tottenham Court Road

A sales message at the foot of the poster notes: "The parlour has got a door."

Otter's Pool near Aldenham, 1797. Little Otter's Pool was on the river at the bottom of Water Lane, on the map, left. The 'Fighting Cocks' tavern was nearby from where boats were available for hire and could be rowed to Bushey Mills.

The Brentford to Boxmoor section of the canal was opened by 1798 and to Braunston by 1805 heralding prosperity and a better living standard from the transport of goods (particularly coal and slate) over long distances. Coal landed at Cassio Wharf enabled the establishment of Watford's gasworks several years before the advent of the railway. This is between Hunton Bridge and Grove Mill Lane.   *c1905*

Horses work best when pulling in straight lines; the horse, above, must have hated the bends and sweeps of the canal, where the pull is against its side, although the helmsman could make life a little easier. Nowadays the canal and its towpath are leisure haunts for fishers and walkers—and the occasional cyclist. Whenever a pleasure boat draws into a lock there's frequently a crowd happy to stand and watch the techniques of filling or emptying the lock before the voyage can continue.

There have been activities upon the canal's waters since 1798, just over two hundred years.

Then it was the 'magic' which shipped raw materials and manufactured goods over long distances hitherto very difficult. The Grand Junction Canal connected London to Birmingham with a length of one hundred and thirty seven miles; the first section was from Brentford to Braunston. Passing through the lands of the Earls of Essex and Clarendon, the towpaths had to be built on the side farthest from the stately homes. No mooring-up or trespassing on their Lords' grounds. The first boats were pairs of 'narrow' boats, a term still in use (as are many of the early boats). The carriage of coal beyond Lady Capel's Wharf (between Hunton Bridge and the Park) was at first prohibited, but permitted in 1805 when a resident tax collector allowed passage of coals to points south of Watford on payment of Coal Tax.

Despite the advent of the railway the canal enjoyed good business for many years, but by 1890 the duty was abolished by which time the railway companies were successfully competing for the boats' cargoes. A canals' merger was formed, and the Grand Union Canal Company was the result; long overdue improvements were made, in which Lady Capel's Wharf was removed. During the canal's heyday John Dickinson was among those who had built their enterprises alongside the canal where barges brought coal and raw materials for his paper-making factories, and took away the finished products. The service may have been slow but for an age which superseded those when there was nothing except the laborious journey by horse and cart, over vile roads, the mass and bulk which could be delivered helped the prosperity of the towns and villages alongside.

Canals restricted businesses to those with access to the waterside wharves; the later railways were restricted to servicing firms near a rail spur, and large enough to warrant sidings into large plants, such as Odhams and Benskins. Only roads were eventually able to give impetus to other firms.

Cassiobury: View from the North West   J M W Turner

Cassiobury . . . and why it came to be sold

Modern history of Cassiobury starts with the grant of Cassio, by King Henry VIII to Richard Morrison in 1545, after dissolution of the Abbey of St Albans. Richard Morrison, who was subsequently knighted, was the son of a Yorkshire father and a Hertfordshire mother. He began the building of a large house and, in the service of Edward VI, was Ambassador to Emperor Charles V, dying in Strasbourg in 1556; the work on the house was later completed by his son. The Morrison line continued through two Charles'. The premature death of two sons meant that the male line ended in 1628 and thus passed to Elizabeth Morrison, surviving daughter, who married Arthur, Lord Capel of Hadham, (later beheaded at the Tower, 1649). Their son, Arthur, was created Viscount Malden and Earl of Essex in 1661; he died in the Tower in 1683 and was buried in Watford. The Second, Third and Fourth Earls take us to 1799; all of whom are buried in Watford in the Essex Chapel.

This recent history starts more specifically with George Capel Coningsby, Fifth Earl of Essex and Sixth Baron Capel who was born in 1757. He had the house rebuilt, c1800. It was he who saw the coming of the canal and of the railway; he died childless in 1839 aged 82. The Morrisons and Capels had always been associated with offices of high state. Upon the death of the fifth Earl the title passed to the eldest son of his half-brother, Arthur Algernon, Sixth Earl (1803-1892). It was he who instigated the sale of the Nascott Estate, of some 150 acres, c1857; it was he who, in 1890, offered 8 acres of Harwoods Farm for the West Herts Sports Club ground, on a 21-year lease, at £100 per year, with a further option of 21 years, and an option of purchase during the first 21 years for £6000. At this time the Cassiobury estate was still intact but was to change. Upon his death in 1892 the title of Seventh Earl passed to George Devereux de Vere, Vice-Lieutenant of Hertfordshire and Aide-de-Camp to the King (Edward VII). He had one son by his first marriage (Algernon George de Vere), and two daughters by his second marriage, to Adele, daughter of Beach Grant of New York. Adele was a wealthy heiress whom he married in 1893; they were greatly feted on their journey through the town, from the station to their mansion in the park.

They realised that 'no repairs had been done for about fifty years' and so started, in that year, the selling of paintings and treasures, whilst maintaining a lifestyle of lavish entertainment for the cream of society. The upkeep and maintenance of the house and grounds was expensive, and their lifestyle vigorous. The first sale of paintings—including Landseer's *Cat's-Paw,* and three Turners—was followed by one of porcelain, bronzes and furniture. Not always occupied, the house was from 1900 available to be let, furnished, for periods of months or even years. Earlier, in 1897, Callowland Farm was sold for development and by 1908 parts of Cassiobury were being sold off, some being bought as a public park. The last entry in the Mansion's Visitor's Book was in July 1913.

George Devereux de Vere died following an accident in London in 1916. Adele became Dowager Countess of Essex and she, together with Algernon who had inherited the title of Eighth Earl of Essex, organised the auction and sale of property in 1922; Adele died shortly after the sale.

The estate comprised some 870 acres. At the auction, in 1922, the mansion and grounds, of 100 acres, and a valuable building estate, making over 433 acres, were purchased by a local syndicate of several men for about £55,000; the West Herts Golf Course, with its 5,000ft of road frontage, was taken in at £10,500.

Four months later the Mansion was stripped of furniture and left; as an unoccupied building, and with no semblance of previous history or glory, it remained so until it was demolished in 1927 and the grounds incorporated into the Cassiobury Estate of roads and houses.

The West Herts Golf Club was founded in 1890 and obtained the lease of a course in 1897. The present course, of about 260 acres, was bought by the Council in 1931 for £24,300, from the Earl of Essex, and let to the Club on a 25-year lease at £900pa, 15 acres being retained for building purposes. In 1935 162 acres of Whippendell Woods were further purchased for a sum of £16,500, with Herts County Council contributing £2,500, thus concluding the sale of the Estate.

Why was the house not kept? The period following the Great War did not permit the luxury of buying large houses because 'they were there'; there was then no National Trust and, if there was, it would have been doubtful if they could have been interested in the house without the grounds in which it should have been situated. As can be seen from desultory prices realised by the sale, little interest was shown. The way it finished meant that Watford, in the long run, had the better bargain.

The Essex line continues, but with no connection to Watford.

At the time of this drawing, by Buckler in 1832, the name of Watford's long road was simply 'Watford Street' as, apart from very short Church Street (by the Church), New Street (a short street behind Market Place shops), Water and Loates Lanes, there were no other roads off. It was only after the opening of estates and the building of new roads that 'Watford Street' gained an element of importance and so became known as the 'High Street'.

This did not take place until after King Street was opened in 1851; Queen Street in 1860 and Clarendon Road in 1864. Market Street belatedly followed in 1889. These streets merely served housing estates. It would be another hundred years before Watford got a new road to connect the town to the outside world—the 'M1 Link Road'—in 1993.

In the drawing, the road across from the church gates to Loates Lane is shown as paved.

Above: Dame Fuller's 'Free School' next to the Church, founded in 1704 (here drawn in 1830), gave way in 1884 to the 'Endowed Schools' in Derby Road, and then to the Boys' and Girls' Grammar Schools, the Girls' in 1907 and the Boys' in 1912.

The Market Hall, with the Town Pump on its right, in a wintry setting in 1832. The Market Hall was destroyed by fire in 1853 and not rebuilt. In its stead a Corn Exchange was opened adjacent to the Essex Arms.

The Birmingham to London railway was not permitted by the Earl of Essex to follow the line of the canal but had to be routed through fields to the north-east of the town hamlet and away from Cassiobury. This drawing shows Watford Station on the 'wrong' side of the road to St Albans. The Station was moved to its present site when the Junction was built with a branch to St Albans; later a line to Rickmansworth was added. The railway bridge was lengthened in 1871 when the third and fourth rail lines were added. The inset shows the Waiting Room (in front of the tree in the drawing) in its modern use.   Inset 2004.

The Silk Mill Inquiry; the Railway is built . . .

A parliamentary Committee sat in 1832, hearing statements about the lives and hardships suffered by women and especially young children, who were employed in Watford's Silk Mill. The mill built by Thomas Deacon, of Wiggenhall, c1770, was leased to Edward Crutchley. Later it passed into the ownership of Mr Paumier and by the 1820's to Thomas Rock Shute in whose ownership the mill achieved the status of being subject of an inquiry, and Bill, to regulate the Labour of Children in the Mills and Factories of the United Kingdom. The mill was Watford's first 'industrial' capacity. Children as young as six, but on average eight years, were employed.

The enquiry revealed that children worked in Mr Shute's mill from six in the morning until seven at night, with a half-hour break for breakfast and a half-hour break for dinner. But no teatime. At times the children were beaten to be compelled to do their work. The work, nearly all standing, was very fatiguing and Mr Daniel, who worked in the mill, was examined; asked about accidents he replied that:

'Saturdays there was always a number of accidents but generally trifling, being rarely more than the the the end of a finger or fingers. That is as far as it relates to the cleaning of machinery at the time specified'. Mr Fraser, examined, remarked 'They do not allow any person to examine those mills except to have business' and of 'James Naylor who lost two hours one morning was deducted 7d of his wage'. Free time was only on a Sunday, and children were disinclined to travel to the hamlet for schooling; few could read or write. If a child was found with a book it was taken away.

A Factory Act of 1833 barred children under nine years of age and those between 9-13 years were restricted to 48 hours; for those between 13 -18 years up to 69 hours a week were permitted.

In 1830 two routes for a line from Birmingham to London were proposed. That passing through Watford was chosen, but objections from the local lords meant that the line could not follow the natural, easy, route as had the canal. It had to avoid the lords' parks. This involved the digging of a long tunnel and the building of a long and high embankment over marshy ground, and a series of arches over the entrance roads at the southern end of the hamlet—which had a population of only 2,960 between Leavesden and Croxley.

A high-level view of Bushey Arches complete with train and a railway policeman. The high bridge in the background is what we know as Oxhey Road. At the time of opening the railway and until past 1900, it was an accommodation bridge to the lodge at Watford Heath Spring, near the Shoulder of Mutton Wood.

The section from London to Boxmoor was opened on July 20th, 1837. The railway imposed several bottlenecks upon the area; the road to St Albans had a narrow bridge; a bridge which allowed access to the Orphanage was adequate for its day as was the bridge over Water Lane; Bushey Arches was also then adequate. The St Albans Road bridge has been widened; the others stiflingly remain.

Each of these three illustrations show Railway Policemen whose job it was to act as signalmen. A danger (red) signal or flag was shown to a subsequent driver if his train approached within five minutes of the previous leaving; the driver would come to a halt. If the gap was greater than five, but less than ten minutes, a caution (green) would be showed.

The 'police' were stationed at three-mile intervals and, after dark, a lamp showing white, green or red would be used. The policeman near the station also had the task of setting off an 'alarum' to give warning to staff to reach their appointed places.

This 'police system' continued for just a few years until, in the mid 1840's, an electric telegraph was introduced.

At the time of the building of the railway David Downer was born. He was photographer Frederick's brother, and lived at what was to be known as 97 High Street, later taking over the stationer's business started by his father. He had a keen interest in the activities of the town and, very much later in life, wrote his 'Recollections'. They tell, in intimate detail, of a life style of the town around 1850 and later. Many of the names of inns and places are still known to us and it does not need much effort to visualise the scenes he described. Modern comments to help the reader are set in square brackets [ ]. It is perhaps curious that he said nothing about the railway other than the location of the early station; to him the town was but the High Street and he, naturally, confines his memories to the street and its immediate environs. The David Downer extracts from the manuscript of 'History of Watford' (by W R Saunders) are on pages 18 & 19.

David Downer is specific about the bridge over the Colne. In the early years which he describes, it is a simple wooden bridge, with the ford alongside. With the advent of the Local Board of Health in 1854 we may conjecture that a stronger wooden bridge was later constructed which would carry horses and carts and although adequate for a while gave Dr Brett, and others, much to complain of.

A stage coach travels through Bushey Arches to be confronted with the Toll collector. The couple upon the stone are on what is now Eastbury Road, but then Hampermill Lane. Our Oxhey Park is to the left. 1837

Robert Peel, Home Secretary from 1822, wanted to distinguish police from troops, and decided on frock coats and top hats. Watford had a Parish Constable by 1832, and in 1841 a County Force was established at No. 193 High Street. (The premises later reverted to a shop, H A Swann, leather merchant, pic p98). After outgrowing No. 193 the station was moved to Estcourt Road when built soon after 1860. This photograph was taken by Frederick Downer in 1863 at his Loates Lane outdoor studio.

Market Place 1863, looking down the High Street. Frederick Downer was born in Watford in 1841 and in 1861 started in business in photography (then fairly new). In 1863 the Prince of Wales married Princess Alexandra of Denmark and Downer recorded this scene of the Watford childrens' procession halted in the Market Place. To make this picture he would have had to coat his photographic plate with liquid light-sensitive emulsion and, with the wet plate in the camera, make the exposure. In 1863, a Mr Peacock extended his printing business to that of producing a local newspaper—the Watford Observer. Below is given the report that belongs to the event. Without this report, there has always been the question of why? what were they doing? and where were they going? This was Downer's first 'big event' photograph, and the Watford Observer's 'big event' story and after 140 years, they sit happily together. Inset 2003.

In the Watford Observer was reported the details of the Marriage of the Prince of Wales, on March 10th, 1863, celebrated at Windsor by order of the Queen, rather than at Westminster Abbey:

"The spring morning saw a warm sun shining on a town gay with bunting and flags. In 800 poor homes there was a festive dinner to be prepared by a special gift of meat and groceries. The children were washed and dressed and wearing red, white and blue rosettes and waiting impatiently. At half-past twelve the 'Smithies' cannonaded a Royal Salute from their anvils, followed by thunderous cheers from the crowd.

At one o/clock the bells rang out their joyous peals.

More than 1,100 schoolchildren assembled four abreast in the Market Place and proceeded to the Parish Church for a short service. Afterwards, they marched back to their respective schools where they were treated to a feast of tea and cakes. Several hundred children belonging to no school were separately entertained at the Corn Exchange. In the meantime there was a cricket match, games, races, rural sports, such as climbing the greasy pole for a pig and a leg of mutton, for their elders.

Later in the evening, the Recreation Ground in Watford Fields was illuminated, a great fireworks display organised and the bonfire lit, traditional to the British on holiday. Watford had seen nothing like this in its history."

The Observer started by having three of its weekly pages printed in London. Progress was steady and seventeen years later, by 1880, the whole of the four-page newspaper was printed in Watford; by 1883 increased to six pages. By 1896 circulation had grown to 5,000 copies weekly serving an area from Hemel Hempstead to Harrow. *The print story continues on page 62, 63 and 93.*

Recollections of Watford in the mid 1800's . . .

In later life Mr David Downer wrote of earlier days:*"The Market House was built on wood pillars with a loft over. Corn was not sold by sample, but in bulk and the sacks of corn unsold were stored in the loft until the next market day. The 'stocks' were under the side of the market house, facing the High-road. The town pump was at the end and was a large iron box, worked by turning a wheel with a handle projecting from the rim. People fetched pails of water by carrying them by wooden yokes on their shoulders, and milkmen and 'women' used to carry their cans in the same way.*

About 1846 Watford had only one street–High Street–commencing at the Toll Gate near the railway arches, and crossing the River Colne by a bridge, a much narrower one than the present one, and with a ford by the side for horses and carts to go through, and I expect the town took the name from it of Wet or Watford. For passing through the toll gate 6d was charged for a horse and cart, and 3d for a man on horseback.

At the end of the garden of Frogmore House ran a narrow lane (generally full of water) which was the entrance to Bushey Meads [meadows near the river]. There was also an entrance by the side of the pawnbroker's shop, to the Mill Stream, so that anyone could fetch water or take horses down. Most houses in the area had two or three steps to their doors on account of the floods, and also there being no drainage, the storm water ran down and over the gutters. Most of the pavement was Denner Hill blocks of stone [sandstone] and only near the shops. York paving about six feet wide, was laid by the Local Board from 1860, and any owner of property wishing to make up his frontage had to do so at his own expense.

Where High Street Station now is were three small houses, one occupied by Mr Poulton, a leather breeches and gaiter maker; and on the other side Mr Draycott maltster had a yard in which a blinkered horse used to go round under a beam to grind malt.

All the cattle coming to market had to pay toll; the sheep pens were opposite the 'Rose and Crown'; the cattle, cows and calves stood in herds up by the 'Green Man' Inn; and the pigs in pens on the piece of ground in front of Meeting Alley. From the front of Mr Rogers' shop along past the 'Essex Arms' hampers of fruit and vegetables were placed along the edge of the pavement. The Town Crier used to charge a shilling and ring a bell and 'cry' anything that was lost or strayed.

Where Clarendon Road begins, was a large barn, and a cottage occupied by the bailiff to Mr R Clutterbuck, [County Historian] who farmed all the fields at the back, and who had a rick yard where now stands the Clarendon Hall [now under Palace car park].

A pond was in front of Watford House, and at the end a plantation of fir trees; as well as the present pond, one in Rickmansworth Road, nearer the 'Elms' and one in Cashio Hamlet, now the garden to 'Little Nascot'. A little way along St Albans Road was the 'pound', a wood paling enclosure, in which straying cattle were kept until the fine was paid. Where Essex and Malden roads are now was Nascot Park and Mr Greenus' Forest nursery grounds. On the right hand side were no houses–all fields–only the 'Railway Arms' at the corner of the bridle path.

The Railway Station was over the bridge, on the left hand side, approached by steps down into the Station Yard. The 'Clarendon Hotel' was the house now attached to the Coliseum Picture Palace and where the Coliseum is were the hotel stables. [Central Tyre Ltd's exhaust and tyre depot.]

Women and children, after harvest, went into the field 'leesing', that is, gathering up what corn was left; and once a week were allowed by Lord Essex to go into Cassiobury Park and gather up fallen wood. Queen Victoria once changed horses to a carriage at the Rose and Crown. Post boys were always in waiting at the 'Rose and Crown' and the 'Essex Arms' for the next turn. Those of the Rose and Crown wore brown jackets and jockey caps, and the others of the Essex Arms blue silk jackets and white beaver hats. Bakers on their rounds had large dogs to draw their trucks.

The entrances to most courts and yards of High Street were under gateways, with a room over.

Across the entrance to the present Market Street was a butcher's shop, with a room over the entrance, by the side of the 'Compasses' Inn. This entrance led up to a path by the side of the Malting, and went across fields, out into Rickmansworth Road, opposite Shepherds Lodge. The path was called Monks Folly. Most houses had pig sties in their back garden. King Street was the carriage drive to Watford Place, and the public house on the corner [Kings Arms] was part of the old lodge. Where the entrance to Queen Street now is was the stable yard of the 'Eight Bells' public house. In the stable yard at the 'George Hotel' where is now a club room [No. 91, Marks and Spencer's store] were large stables with a wooden balcony along the front, and it was said that sol-

diers were billeted there during the Great Rebellion. *The first Police Station was a private house, now number 193 High Street, and the force consisted of one Superintendent, Captain Kelly, and one constable, who used to be called 'Ducky' as he wore white trousers. A watchman patrolled the High-street at night and called out the time and the state of the weather. He had a watch box, which stood on the grass, near 'Little Elms'.*

Mrs Deacon kept the public house, the 'Fighting Cocks', by the side of the Colne River (near Water Lane), and had two boats which she used to let out for a shilling an hour, and one could row up as far as Bushey Mill."

David Downer/Saunder's "History of Watford", 1930

It took about 1,400 years after the Roman occupation before the natives realised that what they were calling 'roads' left much to be desired. But there was no central organisation for road building and the small towns and hamlets had not the financial capacity to undertake such tasks.

Turnpike Trusts were set up to collect 'tolls' to effect improvements and two such trusts affected Watford, The first, the Hatfield Trust (between Hatfield and Bath), set Toll Houses in North Watford and Hagden Lane and lasted from 1757 to 1881—124 years.

The Sparrows Herne Trust (Bushey Arches and Ridge Lane) existed from 1762 until 1872. The 'roads' were maintained in a better condition although the photograph, above, and others of the High Street, show more realism. The state of the town's roads was a source of constant complaint and a General Board of Health Inquiry heard that 'the road outside the surveyor's residence was better than elsewhere'.

This is looking under Bushey Arches towards Watford. Inset 2004

House owners in the High Street started selling goods from their parlour; home cooked sweetmeats and produce; tinware and ironware, potions and remedies, etc. In 1868 Mr Buck started in business, as bakers, at No 48 and acquired No 50 in 1872. A double front made an early 'big' shop. Later he bought Nos 52/54; (see p34, top). Note the frontage paved as described by David Downer. R/h inset, by Mr Hammick, shows the original property. In 1995 it was Dixon's; in 2003 it was the 'Rat & Parrot'. The chimney is a common identifier.   Below: *Plans for the Cottage Hospital, in Vicarage Road. See p78 for story.*

· WATFORD DISTRICT COTTAGE HOSPITAL ·

Charles . P . Ayres , Architect
WATFORD .

Dr Brett

Dr Brett was born in 1828 in London, and came to Watford in 1850, where he died in 1896 aged 68.

He studied at Guy's Hospital, specialising in chemistry and anatomy. He held a number of medical distinctions and posts but his public offices were equally numerous, and for the people of Watford, greatly to their benefit. He was Medical Officer of Health for the Watford Urban District; Medical Officer for the Union and Parish of Watford; Public Vaccinator; certified Factory Surgeon; Hon. Surgeon to the Watford Cottage Hospital; Medical Officer to the London Orphan Asylum and Surgeon to the London and North Western railway. He joined the Watford Company of Hertfordshire Volunteers (Yeomen) 'as a full private' and became surgeon to the Company, rising to Surgeon-Major. His list of offices shows the great interest he took in the welfare of the town's inhabitants. He knew that education was beneficial and fought strong opposition to make it more easily available to labouring classes.

A workman who had laboured and learned to further his craft was afraid that the spreading of knowledge would cheapen and demean his bargaining position to command higher wages. But Dr Brett, and his colleagues Dr F C Wilson Iles and the Reverend Newton Price, were unswerving in their duty as they saw it – in his position as Chairman of Science and Art Classes Dr Brett was aware of technical education schemes connected with South Kensington; he thought these could benefit Watford. He championed the Public Libraries Act which resulted in the formation of Watford Library in 1871; this was the forerunner of Watford's Technical College (which, in Queens Road, in the 1960's, was burned down and rebuilt for use as a Sainsbury's store). The early library needed a bookplate and he had a large hand in the design of it – the basis and forerunner of the town's coat of arms with the 'Audentior' quotation. He was in the forefront of pushing schemes for Technical Education.

If there were complaints about drainage, or 'offensive smells' from the cattle markets in the Market Place, he was forever trying to get something done to cure the problem. He knew that good food was essential for the poorer-paid, and that growing one's own vegetables was a way to health. He prodded the Local Board into action such that eventually 600 allotment plots were available. Although a narrow bridge had been built across the river it was poorly constructed with the arches detaining rotting weeds and year after year he would caustically remark in his Annual Reports about the need for action to be taken. The bridge was eventually rebuilt before his death. He lived in a large house in grounds off the High Street which, upon his death, was sold; Clement's store and the Parade of shops occupied the site.

It is sometimes said, and believed, that the wavy lines represent the Rivers Gade and Colne; this is not so. In the top third of the shield are the Arms of St Albans to commemorate the long association between that city and Watford; the 'harts' represent the Herts in Hertfordshire. In the lower part of the shield occur two escallop shells taken from the Arms of the Earl of Clarendon, Charter Mayor. The wavy blue lines represent the ford in Watford, and the fasces in the centre denote magisterial authority. The motto 'Audentior' is a quotation from Virgil's Aenid VI, 95: "Yield not thou to ills, but go forth more boldly than thy Fortune shall allow thee." Top: Dr Brett; centre, his design for the Town's Coat of Arms (twice since redesigned); and the1930's to 2003 version below.

In the Market Place near the 'One Bell' an artist made sketches which he transformed into an evocative pencil study. This is from a copy negative of a twice-folded paper print handed down, and much faded at the crease lines. The caption is: "It is seldom that one comes across, within twenty miles of London, such a quaint old market town as Watford, or meets with such diverse types . . ., and pity is taken upon the girl, looking longingly at the silk handkerchief, who wishes she had the money to invest in such finery." c1885/6. Original by W Borough Johnson, published in the 'London Illustrated News', 1890

Cattle Market in the Market Place about 1886/7, the 'ordinary' market taking place at the other end of the Market Place. Street cattle markets ceased by 1928, and in Stone's Alley nearby in December 1959.

Above: *Francis Fisher bought Mr Stone's butchers shop – here just demolished. Just prior, though, he had two olden cottages, Nos 74 & 76, demolished and Watford's finest shop premises built at a cost of £2,337, left, to include a slaughter house. When the debris, above, was cleared the way was open to lay out the road line for Market Street and Percy and Francis Roads. The plots for shops sold at an average of £85. After this the 'Rose and Crown' was rebuilt and lasted into the 1960's before being again rebuilt, as a 'Boots' store, and finally, Nat-West Bank.* 1889

Mr Downer's photograph of 1890 shows Sequah, a travelling pedlar of potions, giving a 'farewell' concert of live music from his carriage. More important is the fact that it shows Merton Road in the background and the light-coloured line just above the heads of the crowd indicates the line of just-laid-out Percy Road. This is a view of the grounds just behind the Rose and Crown which, in a year or two, would be turned into Market Street with streets off, and a fine church commissioned. The name 'Merton' perpetuates that of Merton College, Oxford, in whose ownership the land was. About where the Holy Rood Church now is.

Above: *Aubon's were on the corner of Water Lane; this is a display of prize meats following the South West Herts Agricultural Show of 1892. The road crossings were designed for the convenience of pedestrians but were disliked by owners of carriages who complained that 'they caused damage to their wheels and springs'.*
(See pages 82 and 83 for later illustrations).

Next page: *The centre of the High Street in 1897; on the left the houses (of page 12) show their conversions into shops and the second along is a confectioner's selling ice creams at 1d and 2d. On page 92 the shop on the same spot has a sign proclaiming 'Confectionery Ices and Tobacconist'. On the right hand side*

Electricity—or its effects—has stirred man for centuries to learn more of this mysterious and invisible force, most notable in lightning flashes. Volta invented the first battery cell, the Voltaic pile, in 1796; Faraday in 1832 discovered the forces of electrical induction and in 1833 two German scientists produced an electro-magnetic telegraph system.

In 1837 telegraph systems were devised in England, Germany and America and, in the same year, the first commercially successful electric motor, followed two years later by one from a Scotsman. In 1845 an electric lamp was made with a filament inside an air-evacuated glass globe. In 1850 a telegraph cable was laid between Dover and Calais, and in 1858, one between Newfoundland and Ireland. In 1876 telephones were patented and in 1879 Thomas Edison produced a dynamo for use in incandescent lighting systems. In 1881 an electric tram-line service was started in Berlin and at an exhibition in Vienna in 1883 (at about the time of the photograph, top right) motors and dynamos from one-half to 240 horse-power were on show. In Watford, Henry Rogers was advertising telephone sets in 1889, and in 1893 Frederick Downer was using, in Loates Lane, a gas-engine-driven dynamo to produce electricity for his block-making enterprise.

The Watford Urban District Council wanted electricity and in 1896 a consulting engineer gave advice. Lighting was first considered as 'street-lighting' with some four hundred lamps being the first estimate, but increased to 800. An electricity generating station was built in Cardiff Road by 1898; only three municipal installations in Great Britain were smaller. Existing gas lamp-posts were converted with three new and large arc-lamps installed in the Market Place and one in the station approach. (They conveniently help date photographs as before or after 1899/1900!)

The proposed installation was of three 75Kw sets for night use, and one 25Kw set for day use, but increased from 225Kw to 300Kw and 30Kw respectively. Within a short time private houses were

of the road the small premises of Gardiner's (printers of the 'Leader' newspaper), (although in ownership of Mr C H Peacock since 1896) becoming Mr Peacock's printing works. Later he took over the next-door premises (Lipton's) and the firm continued occupation of both until the buildings were demolished in 1961, at which time they moved a few doors along Loates Lane to restart. 'Langley' is the shop on the corner of Loates Lane and just beyond is the tall town house (No. 97) once the shop of David Downer.

At this time Frederick Downer's offices/gallery were across the road at No. 110; his studios were in Loates Lane. The building on the right, with the very tall chimney is where Marks and Spencer's now is but in 1897 was the 'George Hotel' referred to in Mr David Downer's recollections on pages 18 & 19. This shows decorations ready for the celebrations for Queen Victoria's Diamond Jubilee in 1897. For 1960 see p93.

being connected and in 1922 the early plant was outgrown and a new one built. Three-phase supply was generated of a capacity of 4,000Kw; by 1936 was 36,000Kw. When the National Grid was formed Watford was expected to take its supply from the grid—which charged higher prices; but Watford's plant was selected to add supplies to the grid and thus save the town and consumers money. Within just 100 years the generating-station site is closed, and cleared—a 'regeneration' area.

The year 1888 saw two inventions; that of a car powered by an internal combustion engine, and that of Mr Dunlop's pneumatic bicycle tyre with a separate air-filled inner tube. The bicycle tyre

The Cardiff Road Generating Station in the late 1950s; the coal-fired plant was decommissioned in 1968 and demolished in 1973, being later replaced by a gas-turbine station for stand-by and emergency use, in turn to be cleared in the early 1990's and the site by 2003 a regeneration area.

The 'Green Man' offered hospitality principally to market traders; horses and traps were let out and stabling provided. The building was reputed in 1890 to be about two hundred years old; it lasted until about 1924 when it was rebuilt. It was closed as a pub in the mid 1970's and refurbished as a shop, let to the Eastern Electricity Board until they moved into the Harlequin centre. (The site is next to 'Old Westminster/Maximo' pub, in the corner of the Market Place).

was soon to make bicycles a popular means of transport for the working population for more than sixty years. The motor car was a rather slower starter, although around 1900, and at the other end of the town to these photographs, the Watford Engineering Works were advertising as 'agents for steam and oil motor cars on the easy payment system'. They also offered 'motor cycles, 2hp, guaranteed, for £35'. It was thought that motor cars would not catch on as 'there would not be enough trained men to act as chauffeur-mechanics', and that car owners would not actually drive!

In the meanwhile, in the High Street, in 1898, a very imposing building had just been built and occupied by Mr Clement's new department store. The sale of Watford House, on the site, had not long taken place after the death of Dr Brett. Mr Humbert, at the sale in 1896 four months after Dr Brett's death, described the commodious family house "as a charming old place which has taken many years, all of Dr Brett's life, and his predecessor's (Mr Clutterbuck), to make it what it was".

He pointed out the advantages that no roads needed making, and, if so inclined, the buyer could sacrifice the house and sell the whole frontage to the High Street in a half hour. Bidding for Lot No. 1 (house and grounds) started at £3,000 and stopped at £4,250, sold to Mr Judge. He was asked if he would take the field, Lot No. 2, (farm ground which extended to roughly the line of present Beechen Grove) to which the answer was 'yes'; all being sold for £7,320.

A plot on the corner of Clarendon Road and High Street, on which stood the surgery, was reserved and never built up as the other part of the High Street frontage. It stayed as single storey shops until 1985/6 when the corner was developed into a three-storey block of shops and offices, the main tenant being Laura Ashley's shop on the corner in place of the previous 7x Garners bread and cake shop.

Next page: Lower High Street, taken from near Local Board Road, looking towards Bushey Arches. The white fronted building on the left is the Anchor pub, just past where Ausden's now is. Amazingly, the right-hand house/shop with the two dormer windows exists in the 1956 aerial photograph, p89. 1893/2004.

This view across the Market Place was taken with a long-focus lens; trees hide the corner of Clarendon Road and front Watford House. To the left of the picture is a wall covered with posters and from its front wall hangs its Inn sign 'Green Man'. The white house between it and the far trees was Dr Iles' surgery (in 2003, Maximo Bar). Outside the doctor's house beer barrels for the inn may be seen. The postered wall, with apex-roof above, identifies the Market People drawing, just above the old lady's head, p22.
Before Market Street, c1880-85. Inset; Maximo's, 2002

Above: *Rickmansworth Road and Lodge Gates to Cassiobury Park. By 1900 sale of land had taken place to augment the Earl's income, and time was coming when more would have to be sold to maintain lifestyle and upkeep of house and grounds. The Park was strictly private property only opened for fetes or special occasions, and for locals to gather fallen wood.*

Below: *Ricky Road looking towards the Cross Roads (Cassio Hamlet). A narrow lane bordering the Cassiobury Estate it was at one time called 'New Mill Lane' (c1620-c1750), as it led to the new mill opposite the later Swiss Cottage. At the time of Queen Victoria's Jubilee, and the planting of a tree in the little island green near where the distant figure is, it was called the Park Road. The main route to Rickmansworth was the lower road via Cole Kings and Two Pits (Tolpits Lane), which avoided the one-in-eight Scots Hill. The Earls of Salisbury turn-piked the New Mill Lane as part of their private route from Hatfield to Bath. The house on the right of the road, with geese in the garden, is opposite where the Colosseum now is.*

'The Old Ricky Road' is the caption scratched on the original glass plate; approximately near the Boys'
Grammar School. From the look of the telegraph pole a date would be c1906; about this time Messrs Ashby
and Brightman acquired Harwoods Farm Estate, Cassiobridge Farm Estate and parts of Cassiobury fronting
Rickmansworth Road. The development of the Harwoods estate would be starting at about this time.

The offices of Watford Urban District Council had long been removed from Local Board Road to No. 14 High Street. (Charles Ayres, Architect, designer of the Watford Cottage Hospital, lived at No. 14a, and, next door to his home, the new Fire Station just opened in 1900). The ceremonial occasion is that of reading the proclamation of Edward, Prince of Wales, as King Edward VII, in 1902. The site of the photograph in the High Street, where Gade House is, is almost exactly where 'inverted umbrella' glass and metal enhancement has been erected (1999). The Prince of Wales fell ill and the coronation, and celebrations postponed—leading to riots.

Longley's shop in the Market Place (where Charter Place entrance is). Prince Edward fell ill and his Coronation was postponed; local rowdies took umbrage and rioted, prematurely setting fire to celebration bonfires and taking it out on the organisers of the celebrations by breaking the windows of their shops. Mr Fisher suffered damage to property and was so taken aback by the unwarranted vehemence that he deserted public life. Mr Longley's shops (main one shown) were sacked and looting took place—but in the cold light of day most of the looted stock was returned. The celebrations took place peacefully two months later.

Two years after Mr Longley's stores were hit by riots, he passed away. The stores were bought by James Cawdell and developed with great help from his wife. They lived over the shop and employed 14 assistants; this rose to 50 in 1924. Mr Cawdell bought from Trust Houses Ltd, 1929, the Essex Arms Hotel, one of the largest in Watford, whose premises included the Corn Exchange which had been converted into a dance hall. In partnership with David Greenhill (of printing fame) they had the old shop and hotel demolished and a large new store built.

'Cawdell's' *(p108)* became a very popular store, continuing to hold a deserved place in shoppers' affections well into post-war days. An amalgamation took place in 1950 with Macowards with no outward changes.

There was a flurry of shopping development proposals in 1963; the Co-op and the Montague Burton chain were to develop the old Fire Station site at a cost of £500,000; Clements were to spend a similar amount to double the size of their store, and Cawdells/Macowards were negotiating to build a large shopping centre upon their site and the market space behind. By 1973 demolition works had started in clearing the Cawdells site, the Market, Red Lion Yard, the Drill Hall and various smaller buildings in Derby Road, at an estimated cost of £5,000,000. A four-storey car park and YMCA block was to be included. This was the Charter Place, opened in 1976, with a new Market hall on the ground floor, and extensive underground service facilities for accepting deliveries for the Market and many High Street shops.

The entire site was developed by Watford Borough Council.

Previous page: Wooden framed building just below High Street Station housing two shop conversions of Archer's and Fowler's. They were demolished in the mid-1920's and the land taken into Benskin's, and now sheltered-housing built in 1986. Inset 2004.

Whatever the origin of the town's name, the town could be, and frequently was, a very wet place. In 1903 the High Street still showed rusticity, but with the coming of the motor car, and after the Great War, the land here covered by trees would become a motor garage (Monaco) and to the left of the trees Watford's bus garage. The houses on the left still exist as do the newsagent's and shop next door. Those beyond are under B & Q's The Depot, and those on the right have been demolished.

Looking from the railway embankment towards Water Lane in 1903. In 1966 one would have seen the George Stephenson College in the middle; but in 1999 the whole area is a site for Tesco, from High Street to Water Lane, separated by the M1 Link Road, Waterfields. Inset, the road into Tesco car park

A 24hp Milnes-Daimler omnibus plying between the Junction Station and Croxley c1907 (a service started in 1906) turning from the High Street into Market Street. The bus carries 24 passengers, has solid tyres and is braked by a large block being pressed against each rear wheel; it has poor hill climbing ability!

A few years later and buses have greater power and capacity to have passengers on an open outside upper deck. This at 'Two Bridges', Croxley. The nondescript area to the lower left is Whippendell Road (which, if it could be seen, houses Mr Jones' Menpes Printing and Engraving Factory, later the 'Sun').   *c1910*

A picture postcard of Watford High Street looking from Clarendon Road to the Market Place and which shows Mr Buck's Restaurant, Ballroom and Dining Rooms. On the right is the shop of Wren's—leather and sports goods. In the early 1960's both firms moved to purpose-built premises in Upton Road but neither firm found success in their new site and soon closed. 'Wren House' still stands but Buck's was demolished for ring-road widening. For Buck's see p20; Upton road, p100.   c1905

c1900; Dumbelton's shop (with the blind) is No. 231; the 'Brewers Arms' No. 235. Further down is the Town Mill with just 24 years of life left. All is under the Tesco site. The 'Holly Bush' (228) and the 'Rising Sun' were just above where Watford Field Road is.

Right; a most evocative camera study in Watford High Street, outside where the new Woolworths is, looking to the Market Place. It is of the same era as the High Street view on the previous page.

Below; the 'Horns' Hempstead Road, Cassio Hamlet, showing the cottages which extended to the 'Elms' on the corner of Rickmansworth Road. Some survived the building of the Town Hall in 1938/9 but all have since gone.
The destination of the haycarts is likely to be local but at one time was 'long distance', i.e., making the journey into London where they would have to face the hard climb up both Chalk and Clay Hills.

c1912

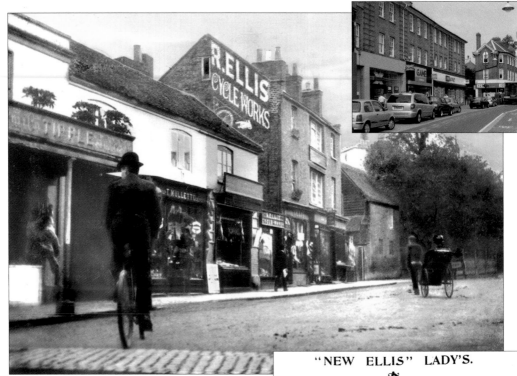

R.ELLIS CYCLE WORKS

"NEW ELLIS" LADY'S.

PRICE £14 14s., WITH TRANSPARENT GEAR CASE.
Or by easy gradual payments by arrangement.

A 'village' scene, but which is our High Street. In modern terms the crossing would be between McDonald's and Gap, and therefore looking to the church. This is about 1905; the trees and Vicarage grounds would go within ten years; the barn-like building once housed Watford's very early fire 'engine'. This is unusual in showing a bicycle being ridden, and a hand-drawn carriage in use.

The bicycle, right, is from Mr Ellis' new range, c1895, when pneumatic tyres were relatively new, they were the best Dunlop, having a five-inch tread. Braking was by a block acting upon the front tyre. A man's racing bike with drop handlebars cost £13; the lady's model with black enclosed gear case was £14. This equates to near £2000 at 2003 prices. In a few year's time factory-made bicycles would fall in price. Inset 2004.

In 1898 William Judge built a handsome range of shops with Dutch-type gables, one with a cupola, on the old Watford House site. Called 'The Parade', Mr Clement and J Sainsbury were among the first occupants. The Parade offered clean shopping away from the more noisome Market Place.

At the turn of the century, 1900, Watford was still an agricultural society, though rapidly industrialising. The iron foundry, sawmills, breweries and the even older industries of tanning and plaiting now saw an upstart in the shape of Dr Tibbles' factory, Vi-Cocoa. This specialised in making chocolate-based sweetmeats, 'in cleanly methods', to produce Mr Boisselier's products. The new factory, in Bushey Mill Lane, was conveniently next to the Watford/St Albans Railway line.

Three years later a grievous fire struck at a weekend, and Captain Thorpe led with steamer, escape and men, assisted by Sedgwicks Brigade and then Bushey, Rickmansworth and Croxley's. Nearly 600 hands were put out of work, two-thirds young girls, many of whom were helping support their families. The fire brigades saved the power house and other valuable stores and the factory was rebuilt to continue in business.

Factories were established in Callowland in Milton Street, Copsewood and Acme Roads, mainly in printing, which started the 'Sun' saga. Off St Albans Road Mr Thorpe's Wells Brewery was well established as was a factory nearby—'Paget's Prize Plates', making highly regarded photographic

Dr Brett lived in Watford House, the grounds bordering High Street and Clarendon Road. On his death 'this most desirable property' was quickly sold and Mr Judges 'Parade' built. Occupiers in 1898 included J Sainsbury and Clements & Co—who gave up in 2004. This sale is about 1910. In the distant grounds is Monmouth House.

Left: Clements closed in January 2004 expecting to rebuild on the site an eleven-storey block of flats. This project failed; the store was sold and rented to T J Hughes, a Liverpool chain of some 39 stores. Store-owner Mrs Rankin wanted the landmark cupola as a memento. It was taken down 18th April 2004.

plates. This firm was later to become part of Ilford Ltd. From Station Road, northwards, the street was a mass of small shops serving every need of the bustling population on its doorstep; from bicycles to clothing; kitchenware to fish and groceries to pianos.

The Copsewood Road and Leavesden Road terraces were built to a price, but with small gardens, safe for toddlers playing, arguably as good, if not better, than many modem compact dwellings — except, of course, there is nowhere to park a car. Bradshaw Estate houses were more costly; reflected in size and quality, and when Windsor, Sandringham and Parkgate Roads were developed, the houses were to be on average twice the cost of those of Milton/Copsewood Roads. The days of the tight and small terrace houses were passing. By 1908/9 the majority of houses in Watford were either new or nearly so, with the exception of old properties alongside the length of the High Street, of which many were in a state of dilapidation.

Residents, generally, enjoyed conditions which would have been the envy of many Londoners.

Opposite High Street Station. Ladies, fortunate enough to have sewing skills, could make their frocks, skirts and blouses with comparative ease; they could knit and thus provide garments of warmth. Men's clothes almost invariably needed the services of a tailor – an expense many found frightening. A good suit was for life; when well worn, it would do as second- or third-best.

Fred Oatley's No. 181 was on the wrong side of the tracks. The wall to the left is that of the bridge of the railway passing underneath the High Street and the Station is opposite. This building was earlier two houses and, like Mr Buck, many years previously, turned into a modern smart double-fronted shop with living rooms and workshops above (this photograph may have recorded that change, or of the premise's impending demise). To the left of the bridge and out of the picture he had large, and much older premises, which almost exclusively sold ready-made working men's clothing, overalls and suchlike. Within just a few years, progress had marched a few more steps; the railway company proposed to turn the single line track into two, to electrify it and run an electric service to Euston. (Trains on this line previously served only Rickmansworth). This duly happened and by 1911/12 Fred Oatley's shop was demolished.

The archway to the extreme right of the picture was New Road. The road sloped down towards the river Colne and was host to a number of small businesses. Among them, later, was County Window Cleaning & Steam Carpet Beating Co Ltd; Hertford Typewriter Service Ltd; Arthur Crawley's car sales and repairs, an abattoir, and a few cottages. All gradually disappeared by the late 1990s except for a Skoda Agency premises. New Road still exists in 1999 but with an entrance a little further south. From the line of the passage, above, a footpath leads to Waterfields Retail Park, inset, 2004; new sheltered accommodation remembers Woodman's Yard in its name of 'Woodman's House'.

Court 21, in c1903, is an example of the dwellings existing along the High Street in alleys and courtyards. The room over the courtyard entrance was taken down shortly after this, and the remainder continuing for many years. Under Tesco's.

Near Watford Fields Road. Always described as 'Court 18, Farthing Lane' one would expect it to lead into Watford Fields but this was not so. Farthing Lane was a few yards further down the Street and when slightly widened was renamed 'Watford Fields Road' and shown so on an 1871 map, and further widened in more modern times. The two little girls stand near the gates of Methodist Chapel, later to become the Town Mission and Ragged School.
In the 1956 aerial photograph on page 89 there is an empty patch on the left-hand side of the road, near the centre of the picture. The scar indicates demolished properties but the Mission existed for another five or six years, until about 1962.

Howland's premises, on the corner of King Street, opposite Harlequin entrance, were previously an under-takers. As a sign of the times a small notice on the wall advertises 'typewriting'. The two cottages have been acquired by Barclay and Company Limited with the intention of turning them into bank premises, which they duly did. In this, the town was served from 1912 until 1998 when the branch closed. Next door is the Cinema Palace, Watford's first 'purpose' built cinema. Seating 500 patrons, it opened in 1911.

L ive entertainment had been occasionally laid on at the 'Wheatsheaf' but the first regular theatre was the Palace, built in 1908 and opened as a Palace of Varieties. Earlier a popular form of entertainment was that of lantern slide shows, as early as 1892 John Ellis and his brother, assisted by Fred Oatley, inaugurated the Lantern Mission in the Corn Exchange. This was later transferred to the Clarendon Hall when as many as 1,500 would attend each Sunday evening.

A surprise was in store for an audience in 1897 when Madame Newsome's Grand Circus, playing at the Clarendon Hall, announced and showed flickering moving pictures. Films, of very short duration, and bearing exotic titles, were presented by travelling showmen over the next few years. In 1901 the first cinematograph pictures were shown in Watford, by Richard Ellis, of Queen Victoria's Funeral. Later, such films as 'Our Navy' and 'Life in our Navy' returned regularly. In 1904 local pictures of Watford and of the Russo-Japanese War were shown, and in 1905 local pictures included a Watford v Northampton Football Match. The Palace showed short films; and the Downer family launched Bipics at the Clarendon Hall. The Corn Exchange ran for a while as the Kinetic Picture Palace (1909 until 1914) when it failed against competition provided by the Central Hall, King Street; the Empire in Merton Road and the Electric Coliseum in St Albans Road.

The Cinema Palace, at 134 High Street *(shown above)* was the first purpose-built cinema; it had no windows (no drawback) but no ceiling; showing roof trusses it was said to be more of a barn. It opened in May 1911 and survived until February 1915. From the turn of the century until about the mid and late 1960s the cinema was unrivalled for entertainment. The Electric Coliseum (Plaza) closed first (1954), to be followed by the North Watford Odeon (1959), and the town Odeon (Plaza, by the Pond) in 1963. The Central Hall/Regal followed in 1968 and the Carlton in 1980.

The Gaumont/Odeon closed in 1983 leaving just the Empire, now renamed Cannon.

The Cannon survived the opening of the cinema complex at Woodside Leisure Park by two years, closing in 1997, just one hundred years after the first flickering images took local people by surprise.

It looks like the makings of a first-class tarmac road — but there is no tar wagon, and crossings are still in use. At the High Street at the corner of Clarendon Road the gravel is being re-spread and compacted, and gravel roads, dusty in summer and muddy in winter, would be the norm for a few years to come.   c1910

In 1891 the town's population was 16,819 and the horse and carriage, and cart, the means of transport. By 1901 the population had nearly doubled, to 29,327; horse buses were in regular service and there had been experiments using an 8hp Daimler wagonette to carry up to four passengers between Gammons Lane (water trough) and Bushey Arches (for a fare of 3d). Popularity overwhelmed the capabilities of the vehicle and the service soon ceased. The motor bus service to Croxley started in 1906 and proved popular. With electric lighting installed in the town's streets, and many more houses being built across the district, there was yet another explosion in population, for, by 1911, a further third had been added to make a total of 40,939. A 2½ times increase within 20 years was straining the town's shopping facilities, and by 1911 motor omnibuses were a regular feature of life, fetching in people more quickly and from further afield.

The intended building of a new bank by Barclays, at King Street corner, indicated the pressing need to offer service to its High Street customers. The street's road surface was also under attack from the multitude of vehicles using it, from lumbering steel-shod wheels of the horse carts to the heavier solid tyred omnibuses, and gradually, lorries.

A tram proposition was aired, from Stanmore into the town and to the Junction, Market Street and Whippendell Road. The problems of narrow streets were insurmountable and before they could be overcome the war intervened. After the war cars and lorries put paid to tram proposals.

Road crossings were still a source of complaint and yet another plea to take them up was made, and resisted. It was stated that 'now the roads are made of granite and well rolled these crossings were not required', but they were left for yet a few more years.

It had taken until about 1907 to achieve a reasonable road surface, but which was still inherently primitive. It was not until 1919 that the County Council contributed a small grant to tarmac the St Albans and Rickmansworth Roads.

The High Street could wait a little longer, until 1923.

There were two former vicarages in Watford of which this was the first and, by 1912, long since disused of its original purpose. Situated off the High Street, through the archway you are looking at Queens Road where contractor's hoardings are around some premises. A new shop is being built upon the corner of High Street and Queens Road for Boot's the Chemists.

Below:
The photographer has returned for an up-date; this time he has gone further into the yard and photographed the old tithe barn, the vicarage obscured by the cart. But rising proudly over the small dwellings and shops rises the new and sparkling dome of Boots . . . The old vicarage was razed soon after and Woolworth's store built. The Boot's dome marks where the entrance to Harlequin is.

c1915

Cattle trading is becoming less important to Watford's prosperity and is seen by many as an offensive and unwanted facet of High Street life. Moves were made to find an alternative place for livestock sales. From 'time out of mind' the market-side of the street was of raised cobblestones to allow drainage. When the markets were eventually removed the space freed was used as a car park, with traffic still using the narrow part of the road fronting Cawdells, as above. The lowering of the road, providing double height kerbstones and making two way traffic, each with its own lane the length of Market Place, took place in 1931.

Outside Sainsbury's, in the High Street next to Clement's, sheep are driven to market; one looks to the Sainsbury delivery tricycle but does not understand the meaning of 'mint sauce'. The tree is on the corner of Upton Road which is where the flyover is. (Inset)   c1910. Inset 2004.

LNWR's Dreadnought Class 'Vesuvius' (or 'Huskisson', according to which source one uses) over water troughs at Bushey in 1899, with an up Belfast Mail/Boat Train. The first coach is for mail sorting and has automatic equipment for dropping off mail at a station into a safe-net, and for picking up mail from a suitable 'hung-out' device.

Charles Brightman, 'developer of Watford' was, in 1890, complaining that Aylesbury builders, with wage rates some 20% lower than Watford, ought not be tendering for Watford work.

His business had been established some twenty years earlier; Board Schools in Watford Fields were now to be built. Mr Robert Ashby, born in Bushey in 1842, worked for Sedgwick's Brewery and joined partnership with Brightman to develop the Bradshaw estate when it came on the market in 1896. The houses they built were larger than Clifford and Gough's of nearly forty years earlier, but were also in the form of compact terraces. After this they bought 35 acres of Callowland Farm from the same source and working-class residential roads were laid out, including Parker Street, Copsewood Road, Milton Street, etc. The properties were small having unit costs as low as £80 each.

Shortly afterwards, plans were made for houses to be built near Dr Tibbles' new works. These roads were Parkgate, Windsor, Sandringham, etc. It was stipulated that no semi-detached house should cost less than £175, and detached £275. Ashby and Brightman were not involved in this scheme, but around 1900 they purchased Harwoods Farm, which extended to Hagden Lane, from the Earl of Essex, and laid out the estate upon which they, and other builders, built the houses. They later purchased Cassiobrige Farm, extending from Hagden Lane to Cassio Bridge and laid that out, including Whippendell Road.

Though these estates were not fully filled-in, further parts of Cassiobury came up for sale and they acquired them by 1908. This was a very large acreage and Ralph Thorpe persuaded the Council to buy part as a park. This was duly done, after much acrimonious slandering of the 'A B C syndicate', which by now included Mr Camp. 65 acres were sold to the Council in 1909, and a further 25½ in 1912. This gave Ashby and Brightman opportunity to develop the remaining part of Cassiobury, for which they adopted a higher value approach for the proposed road – Cassiobury Park Avenue – of houses costing not less than £300 each, a considerable contrast to their earlier houses.

The anomaly of all these transactions is that Robert Ashby finished as a manager for Sedgwicks the Brewers; but all estates laid out by Ashby and Brightman carried a covenant that no alcohol should be sold thereupon, i.e., no 'off-licences' or public houses. The 'Hertfordshire Arms', in St Albans Road, 1935, was the town's first new public house since 1873.

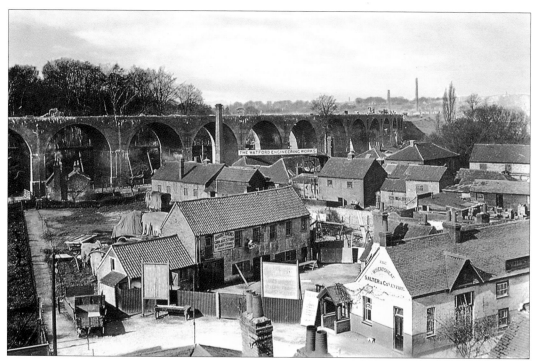

Watford Engineering Works, originally George Tidcombe and Son, was started in 1826. They made the engines for the water pump used in 1854 to first provide Watford with pumped water via a 6" main, from one well in Local Board Road, along the Street, to a small reservoir in Stratford Road from where it served a population of 5,000. The curving viaduct is of the electric railway nearing completion in 1912. (Over Oxhey Park and near retail warehouses). The Wheatsheaf pub will be noted.

A corner of Watford Engineering Works; though carefully posed it is nevertheless realistic in that the steam powered belting is running. The W E W developed a speciality of supplying equipment to paper-makers, filter boxes, strainers and the like.

c1905-1910

Troops going to war along Watford High Street; they are passing the Eight Bells which, when demolished in 1956, became Littlewood's/ latterly Westgate store. Ellis, the cycle repairers (p36), have moved with the times and offer garage services. The bank on the right became Nat West,/GAP opposite Harlequin.   1914

Ralph Thorpe was a Lincolnshire farmer who came to Watford and established a small brewery in St Albans Road near the Police Station. In so doing he started a new career which had a most profound effect upon Watford.

He later heard that the Earl of Essex was selling land and he wanted the council to buy some; other people (Ashby and Brightman) acquired it (for housing) and it was from them that Ralph Thorpe, after many battles, persuaded the council to buy land that we now have as Cassiobury Park. He was a member, and later Captain, of the Watford Volunteer Fire Brigade and attended many fires; a Governor of the Grammar Schools, benefactor to Watford Football Club and during the Great War having the most distasteful task of serving on a Tribunal for Appeals against active service, 'one such lad was appealed for by his mother who had four sons in France; the appeal adjourned'.

Ralph Thorpe served on the Urban District Council being Chairman six times; he was named in the Watford Charter as substitute Mayor to the Earl of Clarendon, was the first Deputy Mayor and the second Mayor of the Borough, serving for two terms. Made Freeman of the Borough in 1927, he passed away in 1929.

His mixture of brewing and apparently siding with the 'development syndicate' earned him much abuse from many ordinary working men. They were afraid that his scheme for the park would increase the rates they had to pay, and benefit only the rich who would most use the park for tea-parties and the like. The Park is the town's most treasured possession. . . and his name is linked with the town's earliest settlers. *(see p60).*

46

Watford was ideally suited for the war's needs. Easy access to a first-class rail system, plenty of parkland and open spaces in which to train, and, with the upsurge of new housing, plenty of houses in which to billet troops. Here some troops are taking a recreational bathe at the open-air baths of the river Colne at 'Five Arches'.   *1915*

The Assassination of Archduke Franz Ferdinand, heir to the Austrian throne, in Sarajevo in June 1914, sparked a domino-effect which was to embroil most of the world. The quarrel between Austria and Serbia drew in Russia in support of Serbia; this signalled an attack by Germany against France, Russia's ally. Britain, and later Italy, Bulgaria, Japan, Turkey and the United States would all become involved.

The steam and industrial ages added massively to the complexity and effectiveness of new weapons of war. Germany, with shorter lines of communications and effective rail systems could, and did, move troops more swiftly than the Alliance. Progress of the motor vehicle, of the aeroplane — and its use of photography for aerial pictures — and the improved arsenals of war in making munitions, tanks, and the means for chemical warfare followed. It was prodigious in expenditure of human life. Soldiers, of both sides, were expected to charge across shell-pocked and barbed-wire strewn fields after intensive barrages. Frequently the barrages did not hit their targets (means for accurate prediction were to come later) and the defenders easily mowed down the attackers. Casualties and killed were numbered in their thousands. It was not long after hostilities started that ammunition started to run out and with a great deal of urgency new munitions factories were built.

Early in the war a munitions factory at Silvertown, on the north bank of the Thames, almost opposite Woolwich, suffered an explosion. The factory disappeared leaving a hole in the ground and windows were broken as far away as St Albans, the sound travelling considerably farther. Strict censorship prevented details from being printed but the story spread by word of mouth.

Munitions factories were established in various parts of the country with local successful businesses given the task of setting them up. In Watford we had the successful Dr Tibbles' Vi-Cocoa enterprise and it was they who were given the task to set up our local munitions works. One, fairly near the junction, and with siding to the St Albans Railway, (extended from the railway to present-day Devon Road), was officially H M Filling Station No 24. In 1917 it produced 113,343 rifle grenades, 390,035 trench mortar bombs, and 458,007 phosphorous and other 4-inch bombs. No. 25 Filling Station, at Bushey Mill Lane, was hutted and filled mortar and other bombs from 20 pounders to three hundredweights (150kg).

In February 1917 a fire broke at the No. 24 Station, and the works' firemen worked to contain the blaze which was adjacent to a packing room containing tons of high explosives. Watford's Fire Brigade men worked with them and assisted in carrying out cases of T N T from the burning building. It was afterwards revealed that 'if the fire had extended it could have been disastrous to the whole town'. Works fireman Thomas Luther Burt received the Edward Medal at the King's hand in Oct 1917, but the town's firemen, Superintendent Pratchett, and Firemen Fountain, Driver and Wise, though publicly thanked by Lord Clarendon, received no other acknowledgement until 1920 when they were each awarded the O B E.

A Great War recruiting drive in the Market Place, in 1915; there's an air of jollity, some ladies eager for their men to do their bit; two lads having a shouting match to each other across the road, a group of ladies with prams. The future, as we know, was to be very different both for those who went and and for those who stayed and had to learn new trades and skills.

Later, Ralph Thorpe and others, upon the introduction of conscription, faced the difficulties of recruiting tribunals who would examine 'for or against' sending a man to serve. Many were the pleas by mothers that 'she had lost sons; this was her last' – perhaps to have enlistment deferred for 'two months', but the day would surely come that the last would have to serve. At first there was pride in the large numbers that a particular family could claim as being in uniform. The excitement of battles turned sour when obituaries grew longer.

Troops in Cassio Road form up for entraining to pastures new; from the pith helmets it looks like Egypt.
A 2yr-old youngster offers a parting gift and Downer's camera records the scene for publication in his latest venture – Watford Illustrated – a weekly chronicle of photographs on four pages of good-quality paper. 1915

After this picture was published in 'Watford Past' in 1999 the 'youngster' (then aged 86) revealed that when he grew up he was told about the soldiers of the Suffolk Regiment, to whom he had given the gift of Woodbines; he has the original Downer postcard upon which his father had written 'July 29th, 1915' and was told by his father, when he was old enough to understand, that their transport had been torpedoed and very few survived.

The war has dragged on; money is needed and so a savings drive, lasting four days, is held and a live tank driven into the Watford Market Place as a morale booster. This tank 'Julian' may have been a prototype before being developed into the British MkV. Armament with one 6-pounder gun in each side sponson (but not in evidence on this particular tank). The crowd looks a little more restrained and serious compared to the 1915 recruiting drive – but £162,020 was raised.   1918

It is hard to realise that several hundred yards away was the Watford Munitions Factory Number 2 (Greycaines); but here troops on leave are helping gather the harvest in 1918 from St Albans Road Field, Bushey Lodge Farm. Bushey Lodge is noted on the map on page 8.

Riverside Road is shown here, c1920/22, as it leads from Wiggenhall Road to the old Silk Mill; the Mill, long disused by 1883, was partly dismantled and the main building turned into laundry premises. During the 1914-18 war years there was no house building or slum clearance and after the war there was a huge pent-up demand. In North Watford a large estate of council houses was built alongside St Albans Road (Harebreaks), where the houses cost more than £1,000 each.

Several slum areas in the town had to be cleared, not slums on account of tenants letting them deteriorate but of old age and decrepitude. Another early estate was to be built at Riverside Road.

'Tommy Deacon's Hill' was a footpath which led from Hampermill Lane (later Eastbury Road) to near the Wiggenhall Bridge. A road was cut through, c1927, and took the name Deacon's Hill.

Watford's Pond still has open space alongside; railings have been put around except for the horses' watering and splashpoint. This is about 1922, the heron, 2004.

The bridge over the river Colne at Wiggenhall Road was private property and Mr Blackwell's man would collect small charges for its use by carts; this view looks at the bridge and to the town. The bridge was rebuilt in 1925 and taken into public ownership. Inset 2004.

A lot of skill that should have returned from the war did not; Kingham's fleet of delivery lorries (mostly steamers), on parade in Clarendon Road, has a good sprinkling of young lads as learners. As with the workers at Watford Engineering Works, earlier, most are wearing suits.   *1920*

Ballard's Buildings are best known for the wrong assumption that they were built in 1836/7 'to house railway workers'. Much older than the 1830s they were, in 1750, in the possession of Mr Dyson – who had a small brewery at the end of the yard – the founder of Watford's brewing industry. His son, and grandson, carried on brewing, and bought a house at 194 High Street, with attached grounds, to where the brewery was moved in 1812. The last Dyson was a bachelor and upon his death the executors sold the brewery, (then Cannons), to Joseph Benskin, a retired publican, in partnership with local draper, Mr Bradley. Benskin's prospered, buying out Groome's (Kings Langley); Healey's (King Street) and in 1923, Sedgwick's (High Street). Water from wells driven deep into the chalk provided water of exceptional purity – hence the name 'Watford Springs' for the swimming and leisure complex built in 1990 upon the brewery site. Benskin's was bought by Ind Coope in 1957 who were in turn bought by Allied Lyons in 1963 and brewing moved to Romford.

New Street runs from the Market Place in the High Street to Church Street. Its claim to fame nowadays is that it houses the pedestrian entrance to Church car park. The little eating house on the corner (p101) would last about another 50 years as would some of the other houses.
In 1958, No. 1 was the cafe; No. 3 a hairdresser's; and Nos. 4 and 4a in private occupation. Court 8, (Ballard's Buildings) of which the plaque may be seen over the courtyard entrance, was demolished in 1926 under a slum clearance order. This was taken about 1914; inset 2004.

Boots' corner (Queens Road and High Street corner, modern entrance to Harlequin) showing apparent chaos. In fact it is a landmark for the town because it shows the High Street being remade and finally given good foundations with a tarmac surface, a smooth finish, and proper drainage. St Albans Road and Rickmansworth Road had been tarmac'd just a few years earlier. Within a few years many public roads would be metalled, but it was a slow process; residents in Gade Avenue, for example, complaining in 1936 that their muddy road was 'Public Quagmire No. 1'. Imperial Way was metalled in 1988, but, in 1998, part of Sandown Road boasted ancient pot-holes. 1923

Several events happened in 1922 which changed forever aspects of Watford's future. Cassiobury House had been empty for some years and the whole estate was auctioned in seven lots. Lots 1 & 2 comprised the home and 100 acres, and a building estate making together 433 acres. Lot 2 was Little Cassiobury, Lots 4 & 5 were pasture lands, Lot 6 the West Herts Golf Course and Lot 7 Whippendell Woods. The contents of the house were sold; a syndicate bought much land to be turned into the Cassiobury Estate of houses; the West Herts Golf Course, of 261½ acres, was taken in at £10,500. The house stood empty. In just over a quarter of a century the late Earl had sold Callowland, Harwoods Farm Estate, Cassiobridge Farm Estate and extensive tracts of Cassiobury Park, of which the Council were wise enough to buy 75 acres.

Meanwhile, downturn had hit trade and a buyer could not be found for the Watford Manufacturing Co's new large factory; the firm was wound up, as was Mr North's Magneto works in Whippendell Road. On the brighter side a new firm called Scammell started in Watford with a workforce of 60 making lorries, and the Watford to Euston line started running electric trains. (The line had been completed for a few years but was worked with steam trains.)

The Council were excited about the rosy future that would attend its plans for prosperity, for the town was on the threshold of being granted Borough Charter status. This was an event which greatly increased the status of the town, though meaning little to the average resident. Radio was new with the starting of station '2LO' of the British Broadcasting Corporation, (an association of wireless apparatus manufacturers), who had received a licence to broadcast.

A tender of £25,630 was accepted to rebuild the High Street, and Watford Football Club got its Vicarage Road new ground upon the site of an old gravel pit. Mr Brookman established a Motor Garage in St Albans Road, (later Tuckers, who moved from 134 High Street; ceased 1970/71).

Unsold, Cassiobury house was demolished in 1927.

Dr Tibbles' Vi-Cocoa works was built at the turn of the century in Bushey Mill Lane between the railway line to St Albans and Sandown Road. After a disastrous fire, 1903, the building was put back into use; post-Great War they misjudged the demand for their products and went ahead to build the large multi-storied factory. No demand materialised and Watford Manufacturing Co went into liquidation, the factory left empty. The 'industrial estate', top, is Greycaine's Estate and the road is the Watford by-pass. c1925/6

The Watford Manufacturing Co's building bankrupted the owners and stayed empty for years until taken over by an American firm to make rubber hose (tubing). In due course the block of single-storey buildings *(shown above)* would be taken into use as a Government Training Centre in the 1930's, attracting from all over the country workless men for retraining with engineering skills. Many stayed on in the locality in employment causing resentment that 'they were taking jobs from local men'. (Those who were trained, whether they worked in Watford or returned to their home area, would put their skills to good account in a few year's time to man the effort to re-arm to ward off the threat from warlike Germany). At the other side of the road, and railway, is the munitions factory, which, after war's end was part turned to manufacturing clothing; later becoming fragmented and let into units as the 'Greycaine's' estate. Sandown Road gained the name 'Delectaland' from the chocolate works of Dr Tibbles.

The field which looks as if it is ploughed is interesting in that the 'furrows' are not. On the original print the straight lines faintly show what look like narrow gauge railtracks which may indicate that the site was used during the Great War as part of the munitions work, and was later cleared. As with the rest of industry, workers will have walked, or cycled, on their work journey.

In the background is the sweep of the Hendon to Hunton Bridge by-pass. This was built to take traffic away from the town centre and for a few years the number of vehicles which used it may have made a slight impression upon the town centre. However, gradually and imperceptibly, the reverse happened. The road attracted building estates, then industrial estates. The residents and workers needed to live, and shop, in the town and, far from easing congestion, within ten years the situation was immeasurably worse than hitherto.

Watford could see no end to the prosperity it thought it was creating, and many years later, when strong measures were needed to alleviate problems, there was never any money in the kitty.

As with other tailors in the town, Albert Ashwell was a gentlemens' outfitter and tailor. He had shop premises in the market place; the firm's heyday was during 1914-18 when they were to tailor many officers' uniforms. Their workshops were situated in a courtyard off the High Street just behind Midland Bank premises, (next to modern Charter Place entrance), but by the early 1920s the buildings had run their span of practical life; a place was needed to get the cramped Market out of the High Street where it hindered traffic; Chequers and Ashwell's Yards were cleared and, in 1928, the Market moved. (Inset, 1995) c1922/5

Watford-born Joyce Franklyn penned these notes in 1995; the little shop 'Archers' of which she writes is shown on p31 and the High Street area on pages 88 and 89.

"I remember in the late 20's, much of 'Lower High Street' for that was where I spent a lot of time visiting my maternal grandparents. They lived in the first house one comes to in Local Board Road – where the Pump House is now situated. After No. 1 came two cottages, then the larger house beyond which was an enclosed property we called the 'Waterworks' hence the name of the Pump House Theatre today. No. 4 was a smart place then, called the 'Red House'. It was owned by a bank manager and his family; their little boy Philip was my playmate and I used to call him my 'sweetheart'. But his mother was rather 'posh' and would make it clear that she was not too happy with her precious offspring associating with a rather scruffy little girl whose socks were forever falling around her ankles.

My grandfather's house was an interesting property with two large gates to one side, opening into what we called the 'Cart Shed' for instead of a car it housed a pretty little trap to which Dolly the pony would be harnessed to take us on sunny summer evenings for leisurely rides around Watford's leafy lanes. Facing Local Board Road was a large flour mill, and although only a toddler, I can remember the excitement with which my elders discussed the night when it was gutted by fire. The shell of it stood for many years after

Where now is the entrance to Tesco's stood a public house called 'Leatherseller's Arms'. It had a nice little garden at the back where we kids could play while our elders took a little refreshment. I remember one occasion when we managed to place an upturned bench against one of the wooden tables to make a super slide, and the tearing of my best silk dress during the fun.

Travelling further to the rear of the pub we came to a sizeable piece of land belonging to my grandfather where he grew fruit and vegetables and reared a few chickens and pigs—the latter he

This aerial view shows, near the bottom, Clarendon Road Corner and along into the Market Place where a Saturday street market is in progress. At the right edge, centre, is a crowd at the cattle market saleground of Stone's Alley, tucked away behind the Compasses and small buildings in Market Street. The Post Office building had not then been built. At the top of the picture is, on the left of the Street, Boots' premises, and on the right, Barclays. Taken in 1922, this photograph shows very clearly the 'large village' character of most of the town centre homes and shops.

would sell to Dumbleton's, the family butcher next to the Leatherseller's. His 'garden' as I called it, was bordered on one side by a shallow but fast flowing stream—the mill-stream—(which runs through Tesco's grounds today).

In the stream thrived an abundance of crayfish or 'crawley-bobs's as we called them. They looked and tasted like miniature lobsters – delicious. There were several other small pubs nearby including the Fox and the Swan, now all gone.

My grandfather worked for Benskin's Brewery as did two sons. Looking back, he must have slaved, one way or another, for every hour that God made. After grooming those huge shire horses he would drive them to the outlying ale-houses to deliver the great barrels of beer, taking all of a long day on the journey that a modern lorry would accomplish in just a few hours.

I would run errands for my grandmother – perhaps to 'Archers'. a little shop near High Street Station that sold hot faggots and pease pudding to take away in a basin; then a little further up, Lipton's of the tea fame. On the right hand side of the High Street, just before Queens Road was the forerunner of Marks and Spencer's, called the 'Penny Bazaar' – a good source for buying Christmas presents from my meagre pocket money. Further up still, on the left hand side, was the open market. I remember being taken there once after dark (or perhaps late one day as the nights were drawing in) and the stalls had naked flares lighting up their wares. But perhaps that may have been my childish fancy and they must have been gas-lights.

Right opposite was the 'Essex Hall' where my parents used to go the occasional elegant dances— my mother in her fashionably short dresses. Too short, as some of my school-friends relayed to me. Apparently their rather more staid mums were quite shocked. I never knew whether to be proud of this information or acutely embarrassed. Thus far up Watford's High Street was the limit of my childish horizons.

The upper part featured largely in my teenage years."

After the Great War the top end of the town was little changed. But portends are here; the Pond has been railed and the surroundings prettified – a state the town enjoyed until the early 1970s. On the right is a market garden and nursery, soon to be sold for building, and the trees hide Elmcote, also to be sold for development. A block of shops would be built in the 1930's, with the Plaza Cinema, Electricity and Gas showrooms. The ladies are walking where a service road would later be.   About 1924/ inset 2003.

The Central Hall Picture House (here, 1926) was opened in King Street in 1913 to join the Electric Coliseum in St Albans Road, and the Empire in Merton Road. It lasted as a cinema, changing name to Regal – New Regal, until 1968 when converted into a Bingo Hall. The Plaza, on the site above in 1929, had a name change to Odeon in 1936 and survived until 1963 when it was demolished and turned into Cater's Supermarket. The Gaumont was built in the High Street in 1937 and had a name change in 1964 when it took the old Odeon name from the demolished cinema.

The Odeon closed in 1983, not for want of business, but because the land was needed to provide space for Sainsbury's store, dispossessed of its Queens Road site. The nearby short service road, Gaumont Way, behind the Parade shops, commemorates the early cinema.

Christmas and Co, established in 1827, were in business as coachbuilders at 141/3 High Street where Harlequin now is, two doors up from Boots' entrance. When they wanted to expand, most street-frontage sites were taken and they moved into, and behind Clock House, in the High Street, when built in 1923. Eventually the bad access and heavy traffic made life difficult. This was not a solus problem. Later it was to affect Benskin's in a similar and more dramatic manner.

1928; this wintry scene is the bottom of St Albans Road looking past the two vehicles to the AA man on point duty; a reminder of life on foot, before cars, car heaters, and gritting lorries.

At the end of 1934 plans were proposed for King George V's Silver Jubilee celebrations by levy of a special rate. A reader retorted to the WHP that over the past few years, with a million dead from the war, millions unemployed and those employed suffering wage cuts, the working class was paying a very high price for patriotism.

The unemployed were to be offered a 5/- meal ticket (married man) and a 2/6d ticket for a single man. The Mayor hoped that all 'should throw aside their usual dignity and make it a real joy day'. The reader suggested that the Council should raise their offer from 5/- to 10/- and make sure that no one went hungry, short of clothes, short of coal or would be evicted from Council houses in the coming winter, and, 'the hungry stomach and ill-clothed body does not provide a very grand or inspiring foundation upon which to build the edifice of patriotism'.

'Meal tickets' were redeemable only at participating food shops.

Some of the flints found on a building site, just off Eastbury Road. They were declared by British Museum experts to be about 12,000 years old. Shown is a hand pick with three planes and a borer. A settlement must have worked the site for a long period of time.Shown slightly smaller than life-size.

Dr Norman Davey, B Sc, A M Inst C E, was a Director of the Building Research Station, Garston and lived in Eastbury Road. In March 1930 he wrote notes of some interesting finds he had made. He stated that, since 1926, he had collected from a small area of land in his possession, situated in Oxhey, a considerable number of worked flints. *"The site is upon an estate which is rapidly undergoing building development, in Eastbury Road, where the ground slopes away gently to the west to the river Colne, and near a tributary of the Colne which flows through Oxhey in a south-easterly direction. The soil was light and inclined to be sandy with a subsoil of chalk.*

"The implements, many of which are of crude workmanship, are of various types and are found generally thinly about nine inches of the surface. They include hammerstones, "pot-boilers", cores and flakes, and there is little doubt, therefore, that the site was inhabited and that the manufacture took place upon it. No. 1 is similar in size to the Thames pick type which is characteristic of the period of Le Campigny industry. Also discovered were borers, arrow and harpoon heads and various specimens which would have been used as planes. A variety of scrapers were found. Nos. 2, 3 and 5 have been found and their form suggests that they may have been used as planes.

"Sent to the British Museum for inspection, the Department stated that the implements were of the accepted microlithic class assigned to the end of the Paleaolithic period and after. Further, of the two groups chiefly recognised, they evidently belonged to the broad-blade industry associated with the 'Tardenois' industry of Belgium, and not to the narrow-bladed industry connected with the 'Asil' industry of France, which is supposed to be the earlier.

"The British Museum Authorities also considered that, on the whole, the group submitted was probably somewhat late in the series, which is supposed to cover one or two thousand years beginning about 10,000BC."

Dr Davey had previously discovered evidence of a later Belgic settlement at Hampermill (but now under the lake). The flint site, Thorpe Crescent, gave firm indications that man had lived and worked there some eleven or twelve thousand years ago. The travellers would have walked from the Belgic area of the continent, there being no 'Channel' to cross. Flints were essential tools for dressing skin, carving bone, cutting and shaping wood, and for use as arrow and spear heads etc.

Flints were not the most important matters on Watfordians' minds in 1930. The American Depression of 1929 had hit hard. Alderman Thorpe had not long been dead; his loss was keenly felt.

The Daily mail reported, in September 1929, 'that they have an ambition to build a model town at Watford.' "By careful planning on scientific lines, exactly how and where all building is to take place for the next fifteen years or so, we hope to create a town distinctly more pleasant and better ordered than it is now" – explained the Mayor, Alderman Hemmings. A population increase of 15,000 to 20,000 was expected. In one big zone, (Cassiobury) houses were to be six to an acre, costing about £2,000; near the railway a large tract is reserved for factories. A field to the north of the town has been suggested for an aerodrome (Leavesden).

1930 opened with rowdy scenes between local men and Welshmen at the Ministry of Labour's Training Centre in Callowland and resulted in two locals being arrested. A petition was organised protesting at the building of council houses in the Eastbury Road locality, and there were protests about a 'bus war' when the High Street was described as a 'race track' and timetables 'are as valuable as first editions'. A lengthy inquiry permitted three operators to have licences but with route restrictions. The Market having been removed from the Market Place, the resultant space was being used by cars parking; and their reversing into the highways caused inconvenience to other users. Watford's Council approached County Council who were distinctly unhelpful.

Six locals were summoned for riding bicycles in Cassiobury Park and each fined 5/-

A bombshell was dropped in June when it became known that the Essex Almshouses (which were in need of repair) were under consideration by the Council to be pulled down and the land used as a car park.

"The attic lets light through, and the walls are crumbling but that does not worry the inhabitants overmuch, for they never use the attic except for storing coals and storage; they live entirely on the ground floor."

In the meanwhile, a fire at Woodwaye in Oxhey revealed that fire hydrants had not been supplied in the then newly laid out road, (1925), and that "the Corporation should have a hard and fast system whereby hydrants are put in at the earliest opportunity and regularly tested in these days of tarmac and tarspraying".

It was proposed to build new indoor baths; this started another long-running debate.

The Almshouses question dragged on through 1931 until August, when the Council capitulated and said that they had no interest in the site; but that repairs would not be their responsibility. (Later a Mayor's Appeal was launched and by January 1932 the appeal for £800 had reached £622; repairs were done by September, but costs increased and by October £944 was raised.)

New sewers were laid in the Market Place, and old wells discovered, filled in and covered, the road layout changed, the Essex Arms demolished; Timothy Whites and Taylors and Cawdells and the Market Arcade were built.

Proposals were submitted to demolish slum property in many spots including Red Lion Yard, Loates Lane, Grove Circus, Wells' Yard and Chater's Yard. Mr Cox, Medical Officer of Health, at an Inquiry, explained that premises were damp, lacked proper ventilation, some had no separate water supply. Protests were received from tenants against the proposal to rehouse them at Leavesden Green in new houses, as this would entail them with considerable extra expense in travel costs amounting to, in some cases, 2/6d per week. Many of the demolition proposals were agreed, most notably that of Grove Circus (about where buses stop at rear of Charter Place).

When Thorpe Crescent was laid out the houses were rather more simple than the luxury Harebreaks site of just a few years earlier. These were two or three-bedroomed and were of the 'non-parlour-type'. (A living room and scullery and bathroom, a coal cupboard was indoors, under the stairs, and the toilet was outside the back door in the porch. Gas and electricity was provided, paid for by prepayment slot meters. The houses were modernised in the mid 1960s).

A 'new' house was not always a blessing. To uproot people from their lifetime's home, which they had learned to afford, near work, near friends and near their religious centres, was for many a catastrophe. A larger dwelling needed new furnishings; electricity payments would be something new; their gas payments might be the same, or thereabouts, but their coal bill would be greater. Most new houses had a garden which needed upkeep and they had to find routes and expenses of travelling to work; to the town for shopping – which would have involved frequent trips in days before refrigerators; worse, loss of contact with friends and relatives. It is easy to understand why some tenants wanted to stay put for as long as possible when a future held terrors of the unknown.

1935 ended with a traditional bad flood.

Although the by-pass, shown here, had been built for several years, the progress of lorries, with severe load and speed restrictions, meant that any firm considering a site for a new factory would put rail links first. This shows Odhams' new factory in 1936, next to the St Albans line with sidings running in from that line. There is space occupied by about fifteen 'senior management' cars and about 20 cycle sheds for the workers, many of whom walked, or travelled by bus. At the top right edge are Eastlea and Westlea Avenues.

In 1816, James Perry, of Uxbridge, applied for a licence to print in Watford (and a poster exists stating 'Printer to the Earl of Essex, the Earl of Clarendon &c, &c' and dated as 1820). His address as 'Printer, Engraver, Bookbinder, Librarian, &c' was Market Place, Watford.

John Peacock applied for a licence in 1827; lived in the Manor House, (242 High Street, on the corner of Farthing Lane), in 1841, and later had a small printing business in premises where the High Street Station is. He later moved to Queen Street from where, in January 1863, Samuel Peacock started the 'Watford Observer'. The paper was born, continued to thrive and, although no longer owned by any local interests, has seen off all the competition. In course of time other printers were to arrive and serve the town, as general printers and as newspaper publishers. None had any great impact apart from serving local people in a parochial manner.

The foundation of Watford's once great printing fame started with André & Sleigh, in Bushey, in 1890. The name changed to Cassell's in 1895 and the firm moved to Bushey Hall Road; the Bushey Colour Press (Cassell's) followed in 1909. In Watford we had Bemrose and Dalziel, in Milton Road which would become, c1914, Waterlow and Layton, later just Waterlows. In 1909 a Mr David Greenhill was assistant manager at the Bushey Colour Press. By 1914 David Greenhill was manager of, and inventor to, Anglo Engraving.

George W Jones, born in May 1860, served an apprenticeship and, after several moves, started up his own business in St Bride St, London, in 1890, as 'Fine Printer to the Trade', specialising in fine typography. He favoured Meilhe cylinder presses and in 1901 printed *War Impressions*, the first book to contain three-colour half-tones. These were colour drawings by Mortimer Menpes. Jones moved to Watford in 1906/7, building a factory in Whippendell Road where he and Menpes worked in partnership for a year before Jones left, later concentrating on type design and founding.

In 1914 Cassell's (André and Sleigh) and Bushey Colour Press merged, together with the Anglo Engraving Company, London, to take over the Menpes Printing and Engraving firm and renamed Sun Engraving Co Ltd in 1919. In the meanwhile, soon after the start of the Great War, David

The 'Elms', (at the Cross Roads), and its paddocks, was bought in 1920 as a 'good bargain' at £12,250 though this caused much heart-searching of the Council's Sites Committee. A site was needed to build a hospital as a peace memorial. The hospital was built on the stable land and ground in Rickmansworth Road, leaving the 'Elms' available for later use, perhaps for Council or other offices. The 'Elms', shown here in September 1937 being cleared before demolition, had for three years or so been used by the Treasurer's Department. The new Town Hall was in use in November 1939, officially opened in January 1940.

Greenhill was faced with the challenge of producing for the Government forgery-proof bank notes to replace gold coinage. Taking some time this was achieved and the country's first bank-notes were printed at Waterlow's, in Milton Street, just off Leavesden Road – a contract which lasted until 1928. At a talk to a meeting of the Guild of Young Printers, in 1940, David Greenhill outlined progress as: "1904/5 Stone & Cox; 1918/19 Hudson & Stracey (Carey Place); 1919, Bournehall Press; 1919; Gibbs & Bamforth (West Herts Post); 1924/5, Davey & Winterson, North Watford; 1926, Messrs Greycaines [Europe's largest producers of low priced books and novels until 1933]; 1929, Messrs Blowers, 1935 Messrs Edsons and in 1936 Odhams Ltd came to Watford."

David Greenhill wanted to print gravure in colour and so set up a studio in which still-life products could be photographed for advertising. He wanted a rotary gravure machine capable of printing four colours on paper from a reel. Such a machine did not exist; no British manufacturer was interested and he found the same reaction in Germany. Eventually he found an English firm to make the machine 'without guarantee that it would work'. But it did and he had produced the first colour sheets by rotary gravure. The firm was swamped with orders.

He knew the necessity of continuity of work; periodical publication offered that asset and was cultivated. The Sun's masterpiece was the conception and seeing to reality the weekly 'Picture Post', which, with brilliant photography and writing, gave to the reader an insight of other aspects of life, often championing causes against social ills, deprivations and injustices. David Greenhill had travelled frequently to Germany during the 1930's and seen the portends which he found distasteful, and he had no hesitation in using Picture Post to let readers be aware.

During the war the firm's specialised services were called into full play to print the millions of pages of maps needed by the Allied Forces for the invasion and subsequent progress through Europe. The printing business was, in 1945, merged with Hazell, Watson & Viney and included Rembrandt Photogravure Ltd. In 1945 Captain Robert Maxwell (Jan Ludvik Hoch) in Berlin started a career which would plunder and bring down both Odhams and the Sun.

Cox's specialised in making tubular seating and furniture–very suitable for office and factory environments–as an alternative to wooden products. They established pre-war a factory on the By-Pass. Springs were provided by Chiswell Wire Company who were founded in 1932/3 in Sandown Road at the Balmoral Road end of Delectaland. Chiswell's main business was then supplying springs to High Wycombe furniture makers. Both firms were pressed into war production, as were others, and after the war both reverted to their previous roles; but Cox's finished in the ownership of Raleigh Industries. In rationalisation Raleigh's decided that the Watford plant was not viable. It closed in 1967, the premises divided and let in small units.
In the early 1980s, after Croxley Business Park was built, the Cox's site was scheduled for the same 'business park' treatment, but with the onset of recession came to nothing. The site was cleared, and is now 'Costco'.

In 1937 the great Gaumont cinema *(p111)* was opened by Mr Will Hay and a year later the subject of 'Sunday opening of cinemas' was discussed by the Council. A puritanical streak suggested that Sunday opening would desecrate the Sabbath, but that a poll should be taken to let the electors make their choice. Duly held, the result was a massive 9,565 for and 6,908 against; Watford got its Sunday cinemas. There was a sting, profits had to go to charities and it was agreed that the Council ask County Council to bear in mind the claims of the Peace Memorial Hospital and the District Nursing Association. And, yes, the Council suggested that performances should start after the ordinary hours of church services, that the types of films shown should be suitable for persons of all ages, and a condition that 'music must be of sacred or classical nature' be rigidly enforced.

The remains of Watford's historic mill (at the bottom end of the High Street) was bought (and demolished in 1938), and huge plans were made for the layout of the Leavesden King George V playing fields, to include twenty tennis courts, three bowling greens, three cricket pitches, running track, football hockey and netball pitches as well as pavilions etc.

Plans were unveiled for a new St Albans By-Pass, starting on the Watford By-Pass near Berry Grove. (This was deferred, finally opening in 1959 as the M1, when it brought vast problems to Watford). In 1938 plans were discussed to buy properties along a line from Clarendon Road, past Red Lion Yard, along Derby Road and into a new, widened, Water Lane so as to provide relief to the congested High Street.

In a rush 60,000 to 70,000 respirators (gas masks) were assembled by Sun Engraving works, the Model Laundry, the Watford Steam, Millars, and Silverdale Laundries, 50,000 being assembled in ten hours by a total of 600 employees. The public were later asked to go to their respective polling station to have one supplied and fitted.

The High Street, looking to Clarendon Road corner, in April 1939. The 'Parking' problem continually occupied the Council's minds. WWII solved the problem for the next ten or twelve years, until it re-surfaced more vigorously. The 1990s shops where C & H Fabrics and Perring's were, have since Harlequin, been let as 'swag' shops. Now gone, the site is that of Woolworth's.

Work started on the buildings of Watford's new town hall, and a new cinema, Odeon North Watford, was opened. A cattle market and car-park proposal was drafted for the Ballard's Buildings site but fell through with the advent of war. Early in 1939 a bye-law was proposed that would have the effect of ensuring uniform closing time for shops, of 7pm. Most shops stayed open far later than this, giving staff long working hours.

The threat of war had been in the air for a long while. Picture Post had published an article, in November 1938, instancing the pogroms, including 'Kristallnacht' against the Jews, and how, in Munich, 10,000 were rounded up and told to leave within 48 hours, an order later rescinded but not before overwhelming terror was caused.

Air-raid precautions were started, and details were given about the effects of new 'incendiary' bombs which burned at 1,300 degrees centigrade and which were small and light in weight; air-raid shelters were delivered to those who wanted one. Of two types, the Anderson was of corrugated steel which was partly sunk into the garden soil and with sandbags or earth piled on or over; they gave excellent protection against blast. Morrison Shelters, less popular, were, in effect, re-inforced tables under which the shelterers could sleep; the construction would save them from the falling ceilings and roof, etc.

Evacuees were brought into Watford from London and were dispersed to outlying districts, and ration cards were issued. War was declared on September 3rd, 1939 and the Borough Council made provision for providing allotments, and a campaign started to 'Dig for Victory.'

People were apprehensive about the future . . .

War is declared

'What is going to happen; what do we do?'

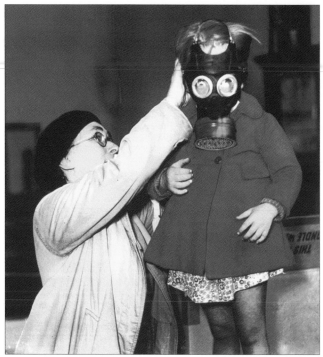

Air-raid precautions were started in 1938 on the advent of a war-scare. A sigh of relief was given but was short-lived with war declared in September 1939. The year's grace had given the country a much-needed breathing space to harness production and training to compete with the might of Germany – who had been extensively re-arming for some years. Gas-masks had been ready for some time, and were now being issued.

The new Town Hall was opened in January 1940, in the midst of the 'phoney war' when troops were impregnable behind the French Maginot Line. The German High Command under arch-strategist, Adolf Hitler, was taunted with songs of 'Run, Rabbit, Run' and 'Hang out your washing on the Siegfried Line'.

Hitler was a thug not bound by conventional rules of war, his blitzkrieg after Poland bypassed the French Maginot Line by overrunning Holland and Belgium and in an amazingly short time had forced the British Expeditionary Force back to the little French resort of Dunkirk. From here some 330,000 troops were rescued by fleets of 'little boats'–a deliveration forever enshrined in our memory; the army was saved, but all equipment was lost. The war was no longer phoney but devastatingly real and was soon to be followed by the capitulation of France. Much of Europe was now conquered and Great Britain, supported by Empire troops, with trepidation, stood alone.

Invasion was feared. Air Raid Precautions became a priority; buckets of sand and stirrup pumps were the standby equipment of the nightly firewatchers on the lookout for firebombs. 'Home Guard' units were established. (They were later to be gently mocked in the humourous series of 'Dad's Army' (written by Jimmy Perry, of Watford's Palace Theatre) but they had the merit of releasing younger men for training for active duty.)

Industry faced the problem that its skilled men were likely to be called up, and training programmes were instigated to teach women the mysteries of operating engineering machinery, which they did with every success. Women were called upon to serve in the Ambulance and Fire Services, and formed the ATS, WRENS and WAAFS, working closely alongside their 'senior' forces, often close to or in the front-line. They left their homes and formed the backbone of the Land Army where their work was vital in securing food supplies. Mobilisation was almost total but not all men were called to arms; 'Bevin Boys' played their part as coal miners.

There was a lull after May's Dunkirk debacle; it was learned that Hitler was preparing an invasion,

'Russell's' was a large tract of land bordering Hempstead Road opposite the Grove. Courtlands Drive had been cut through before 1939, but the estate off not developed. Russell's was used extensively for troop training, as with this Home Guard unit on anti-tank training in 1941. A curious anomaly is that the Sergeant-Major leading the detachment, and the private, perhaps on sentry duty, are expressing concern at the officer who leads and looks as if he is about to collapse . . .

but all he had was a motley collection of flat-bottomed barges totally unsuited to make a Channel Crossing. He needed first to destroy the RAF, which Goering boasted his Luftwaffe could do. It could not, and did not.

Not all available RAF fighters had been sent to France in 1939, many were husbanded against a need to defend our country. The need arrived; the German efforts to destroy the RAF bases was fought off, and in the September of 1940 the terror attacks on London and other cities started in earnest.

Bombs fell in and near Watford where damage to housing was caused and lives lost. Pundits would say, knowingly, that 'they were after the railway viaduct' (to disrupt rail service to the Midlands) or that 'they were after such and such a factory'; we found out much later that the bombs were dropped indiscriminately, though not then seeming so.

In addition to the 'savings drives', (not at first taken seriously) drives were started to collect paper for re-use; iron and steel railings, and aluminium. For most of the first year production of ordinary products—camera films, stationery, clothing, furniture, household goods, etc,—continued with little outward change. But stocks were being exhausted and when gone could not be replaced.

Savings drives came and went; magazines were available only by an order placed, there were no spare copies. They grew slimmer, and then smaller. Newspapers grew smaller, and thinner and by war's end, for example, the broadsheet sized papers were of just four pages. Bananas and oranges disappeared and most foods were strictly rationed. The blackout caused hardships, torch batteries had to be used sparingly, razor blades scrounged and techniques learned to sharpen them for re-use. On the sparse rations the nation grew thinner, but fitter.

War, and its effects, were to last far longer than anyone could have imagined.

It started with biplanes and finished with jet planes, with aspirin and finished with penicillin, with rudimentary television and finished with radar.

Scammell's, in Tolpits Lane, West Watford, were perhaps best known for their remarkable Mechanical Horses; compact three-wheeled tractors coupled to a variety of different-purpose trailers. One is shown here as a self-contained firefighting appliance, being tested during 1938. As well respected makers of 'large-load' carriers their wartime output included tank transporters. Established in Watford in 1922, a later Leyland-Daf merger resulted in closure during 1987.

'Dig for Victory' and rationing were on people's minds. That there would be food waste was inevitable – though it lessened with time – and here the Corporation's pig swill collection is being unloaded at Holywell; collection then amounted to about ten tons weekly to feed their pigs. 1940

Watford, being close to London, suffered indiscriminate bombing, with Trewin's being hit by incendiaries in January 1941. Mr Matthew's draper's shop in Queens Road in 1871 was acquired by Mr Trewin in c1880, moved to Nos.26/28 in 1887; was bought in the early 1920s by Selfridges and, later, by John Lewis.

Tividale's was a small iron and brass foundry in Local Board Road more used to making manhole covers and drain gratings. Here they have just cast in brass a name plaque for H M S Watford, a vessel which was never commissioned. Mayor Councillor E J Baxter, 2nd from left, watched the casting.   1941

This Lancaster had been on 27 operational flights, including one raid on Berlin, and was now relegated to the no less important duty of drumming up interest in savings; here being assembled on the green-sward in Rickmansworth Road, alongside the Town Hall, in May 1943.

Another means of raising money was to charge admission to see this captured Messerschmitt 109, being shown behind Cawdell's smaller shop in the High Street, (now the premises of Lloyd's Bank).   *1943*

In 1940 a 'Spitfire Fund' was set up to raise the money to buy a Spitfire – £5,000. The fund dragged on and when closed had just made the target, but leaving some £85 expenses to be paid. In 1941 a 'War Weapons Week' was held for which the target was set at £250,000, but which raised £1,272,629. The following year was 'Warship Week' which raised £1,225,809 and in May 1943, here, it was 'Wings for Victory Week'. The target was £1,000,000 to buy 50 Mosquito aircraft; £1,150,326 was raised. Troops of all branches of the services paraded at the march past, a Royal Air Force band playing at the corner of St Albans Road and the High Street, with Mayor Alderman Simmonds taking the salute.

In the dark days of 1940 the drone of German bombers over Watford's night skies brought forth the recurrent cry of "where are our planes?". We were not to know, then, that we had no night fighters, and that our stock of fighter planes was all but exhausted from the gruelling Battle of Britain. Before the war de Havilland's pinned their faith on fast, streamlined, passenger planes, but received no Government support.

They proposed an unarmed fighter/bomber, relying on speed. This did not meet with official approval, but during 1939 de Havilland produced plans and on 1st March 1940 received a first order for 50 planes, but with official scepticism. de Havilland understood and built in wood; this was easier than metal fabrication and within just over eleven months the first Mosquito flew and showed its amazing capabilities.

Leavesden changed from components to making Mosquito wings for the Hatfield plant, and then undertook production of complete planes. The High Wycombe furniture industry cooperated. The Mosquito was designed to take four 250lb bombs. The load was doubled before it flew. The load was later increased to 4000lbs and with its superior speed it could deliver its load to Berlin, with a crew of two, in safety. Early Flying Fortress loads, with eight crew, was 4000lbs.

The Mosquito's high speed enabled it to be used for daring low-level attacks with pin-point accuracy. In many roles it roamed Germany's skies at will, even, in January 1943, disrupting a parade being addressed by Reichsmarshal Herman Goering. They later formed the Pathfinder division in which they used their features to lay target markers for succeeding bomber forces to aim at. Mosquito's were made in Canada and Australia. The fighter version achieved successes and, with the aid of Beaufighters and Defiants, broke the back of German night raids upon this country. The Leavesden factory of the de Havilland group produced 1,390 of the 5,584 total production.

The appeal of Watford's Pond as somewhere to stop and stare – for young and old – is made easier with the railing to lean against.   *1949*

suggested a 'citizens' theatre with a parade of shops, exciting public imagination. Later, relief road plans were published *(p96)*. Despite these plans, which showed huge road widening at the spot, the local newspapers and public still anticipated a new building to compliment and enhance the Town hall approaches. A detailed analysis of buildings, density and usage, condition and access; of road usage–where vehicles left Watford after entering, and how many cars were parked and where–was made in 1954 and published as a draft plan in 1956. The conclusion was that there should be an Eastern relief Road, from St Albans Road to Water Lane (which today we know as Beechen Grove).

The property involved caused an outcry, but the outcry did not ease the congestion.

This plan, being too ambitious to be carried out within any foreseeable future, was the forerunner of alternative schemes. The Council wanted to widen King Street to lessen a very dangerous exit into the High Street; County said 'No', which left Watford's Council fuming until they decided that it had to be done–and did it. In 1956 Mr Sage had broached the idea that Clarendon and Station Roads be developed as an office centre: 'Why not a Threadneedle Street in Watford?' and of Clarendon Road as dual-carriageway.

Of plans to develop the corner of Longspring and St Albans Road he spoke of the aim to make St Albans Road dual carriageway to the Cross Roads. Of the Central Area plans (Feb 1957) he explained, in 1958, that car parks would be sited adjacent to the relief roads, and shops would be within easy walking distance and 'absolute safety of the shopping public can only be ensured by the complete segregation of pedestrians and vehicles.' In other words, a complete prohibition of all vehicles entering the shopping area. He was in favour of high rise blocks of flats and suggested them for Sotheron, Sutton and Estcourt roads.

If Mr Sage thought that St Albans and Clarendon Roads could be 'dualed' he was either unrealistic about road widths, or over-optimistic about the amount of property which could be demolished to attain these roads. Of the 'pedestrian precinct scheme' he threw away the concept with 'it would be difficult, though not impossible, to have a similar arrangement in Watford. The Central Plan does not provide for this . . . the new relief road will encourage its use by through-traffic, although still leaving the High Street accessible to all vehicles.' Which is still the situation 45 years later.

South Oxhey 'New Town'

For some the pace was tediously slow in being allocated a new home. For many there may have been pride at being in at the start of a new town. Except that it was not a town but 'merely' a housing estate, owned by the L C C, at first administered by Watford Rural Council until control passed to Three Rivers Council. The 'Totem Pole' near Hayling Road became the landmark to find where the desired road was. In the background, to the right of the Totem Pole, is the Progress Board where the weekly tally of completed houses was recorded. Building started in 1947 with the first tenants taking occupation in the November. Shops were in Little Oxhey Lane by 1949 and house building finished by 1950. Nearly 15,000 people were rehoused. 1949

Londoners had suffered throughout the blitz and most 'stayed put' under semi-permanent conditions of hardship. These problems were greatly increased with the V1 and V2 attacks and it was obvious that rehousing programmes would be needed; it would not be possible to rebuild in London nor would it be desirable to rebuild to the same high overcrowded density as hitherto. Land at Oxhey, in the ownership of the Blackwell family, seemed suitable. Mr Blackwell had just recently died and it was supposed that the land would be offered to the 'National Trust' but this had not yet happened. The LCC wanted Oxhey's land; so many residents in and around Watford hated the idea of so much virgin ground being spoiled by housing that an enquiry had to be held.

It came to the conclusion, of course, that there was no reason why the compulsory purchase should not go ahead. In mitigation for the plan it was revealed that the land lay basically in a slight depression and could not easily be seen from the railway, and that the approach roads from Eastbury Road and Sandy Lodge would 'screen' the estate which would hold some 15,000 people.

For many the traumas of Oxhey, now called South Oxhey to distance it from its neighbours, seemed as bad as the worst days in London. There were no places of entertainment or worship; there were few shops. The houses, of many varieties, were not insulated and had only a conventional fire in a living room; electricity proved too expensive to use for heating. Burst water pipes were commonplace in winter. Eventually, mobile shops made the rounds of the new streets–all largely unmade –and although welcome to a degree there were complaints about the rather higher prices charged for groceries, vegetables and meats. For many the drastic change to a 'house' and quiet surroundings proved too much and meant a return to the London they knew and loved.

South Oxhey's shopping habits included, for many, a visit to Watford, and seen, within the limits of great shortages of consumer goods, as a good place to shop. With Watford's own population steadily rising problems of lack of shop sales-space became more apparent.

Moselle occupied these premises in the High Street, on the Parade, until the lure of Harlequin called and they moved in with the first phase in August 1990. In 1998 they withdrew from Harlequin in favour of premises on the corner of Queens Road and Derby Road. This is Autumn 1949.

The postwar winter of 1947 was one of the worst within living memory; the meagre coal ration doing little to keep the cold at bay. Alderman Last, in Council, asked if the cinemas were keeping to the strict rules regarding Sunday performances. Half a mouldy loaf and hunks of bread were exhibits at Watford's 'Battle of Bread' exhibition–they had been found in a refuse collection. A 73-year old farmer was fined £150 for selling more than the permitted amount of milk. Serving men returned, hopeful for the future, and many found that their previous jobs had been filled, no longer existed or even that the firm had gone! The war's years of uncertainty still prevailed. In 1947 the school-leaving age was raised to 15, having the effect of increasing the shortage of labour; an old-established fishmonger was fined for not showing prices and weights of fish.

The National Health Act came into being, taking in the Peace Memorial Hospital and its grounds. Coal was short; firms had to work staggered hours to reduce electricity consumption by one third; sirens were to be used if power cuts were imminent. Parts of Lea Farm were zoned for industrial use and 'Kytes', Garston Manor, Hillside and Hunton Bridge, were earmarked for housing.

A mains radio–if to be found, as they were for export–cost about £22, inc 30% Purchase Tax (about £600 at today's prices). The corporation used aerial photographs to charge a builder with carrying out work without a licence, the case being dismissed as no proof could be substantiated as to date and time the works were alleged to have taken place.

In June of 1949 there was a bright spot. Several developments arising from the war were hailed as 'wonders'–pens which could write under water, and did not leak at high altitudes (Biro); nylons, and fluorescent lighting, which gave light equivalent to to that of a conventional bulb of about three times the wattage, thus offering brightness, or savings of electricity. The new lights were installed in the town's main streets, almost exactly 50 years after the first electric lights.

Bread, unrationed during the war, became rationed. Ministry of Food officials saw a man offering chocolates for sale from the boot of a car, and this led to charges involving nearly a quarter of a millions personal points-worth (coupons) of sweets. As late as 1953, eight years after war's end, sugar, bacon, cheese, fats, eggs and meat were still on ration.

In St Albans Road the cyclist leaves Leavesden Road; the crowd have just left the North Watford Plaza cinema. The Police Station, on the left of the road, fell into disuse of its original purpose and was used to house homeless families before being sold by Herts County Council in 1961. *1949*

St Albans Road and the corner of Church Road, looking towards the Town Hall; the shops on the left-hand side (and starting with the 'Railway Arms') would, in a few years begin the long gradual period of closures and run-down before being demolished in the early 1960's for road widening. 1949. *Insets 2004*

November 11th; two-minutes silence and the laying of a wreath, at the memorial in Rickmansworth Road. The statuary, by Mary Bromet, is now in the precinct between the Town Hall and Library, p120.   *1949*

Watford was a bustling growing town way back in 1885; estates of Clifford & Gough's in Estcourt Road were about twenty years old, but Market Street and Watford Field's few streets were yet to be built. Queen Street had reached the Junction and Watford New Town was a thriving and busy area. There was a small building in Willow Lane, the Pest House, for infectious diseases.

Into this scene the Watford District Cottage Hospital was founded in Vicarage Road. The population was about 16,000. The hospital had two wards, of four each male and female, a one-bed ward, and a small operating room. To mark Queen Victoria's Diamond Jubilee, 1897, a new six-bed ward and theatre were added, and in 1902, to mark the Coronation of Edward VII, a further additional two six-bed wards, making the total of 27 beds. The Great War showed how woefully inadequate were the facilities–many wounded men being cared for in large homes around the district.

An Urban District Council Committee was set up in 1919, to find a site for a new hospital; that next to the 'Elms' in Rickmansworth Road was purchased on very good terms and a campaign started to raise the money. The Chairman of the Appeal Fund was the Earl of Clarendon, backed by Mr C H Peacock, of the Watford Observer. £90,000 was a lot of money to raise and, by pursuing every means of collecting pennies to pounds, slowly the target was met.

The Hospital was built and opened by H. R. H. The Princess Royal, Princess Mary, in June 1925.

With 87 beds, extensions were added in 1937 making a bed total of 154. The Peace Memorial was taken into the National Health Service in 1946, as was Shrodells. The latter, a Union Workhouse built in 1838, in Vicarage Road, was in 1930 turned into a hospital. In 1984 a six-floor general-purpose block was added and the 'Peace' transferred to the site in 1985; the name: 'Watford General'.

The inadequate Pest House was replaced by the Isolation Hospital in Tolpits Lane c1898. Empty, the 'Peace' grew derelict; part was demolished; the clock was stolen, and outcry raised. The outcry continued at intervals and official hands were stayed from destroying what was left. Watford General was merged with Mount Vernon in 1993 and in 1993 it was announced that the 'Peace' would be turned into a hospice. As the 'Peace Hospice' it was opened in 1996. In 1998 the Regional Health Authority announced that it would like to see Watford General downscaled and merged with Hemel Hempstead's hospital, or replaced; but the wish was stated as denied in 1999.

Clarendon Road late 1949; the police station and court are obscured by the bulk and grounds of the Congregational Church at the corner of St Johns Road but otherwise many properties are the original houses – though some had been converted to office use. Inset 2004.

The Carlton Cinema, Sunday 23rd April 1950; the big film starting on the Monday was 'Back to Bataan' featuring John Wayne and Anthony Quinn, (made in 1945), with 'Bachelor Bait' as second feature starring Robert Young, Shirley Temple and John Agar. At the Palace, 'Dusty Ermine' by Neil Grant.

The Parade, High Street, Watford   *1949/2004*

This is the riverside path through Oxhey Park from Wiggenhall Road to High Street. The ground on the right was part of Wiggenhall Estate and the pill box is a reminder of early wartime optimism that such things could slow down an attack. The next nearest one was in a triangle of land at the junction of Deacon's Hill, Blackwell Drive, and Wiggenhall Road.   *1957*

The brewers were one of the last bastions of craftsmanship, their wheelwrights and coopers still making wheels and barrels by methods handed down for generations. The floats are part of the 1950 Carnival Procession, here passing through Station Road to Clarendon Road.

Horse Shows and Gymkhanas had long been a feature of Watford's Whitsun Carnival. They continued – aiding Old People's Charities – until it was decided, in 1996, that West Watford needed a cricket pitch. One was marked out in the park and it was noticed that part of the show ring would intrude upon the pitch. The Horse Show and Gymkhana was sacrificed. The July 'Rainbow Festival' is the carnival's replacement.

Why 'Water Lane'?

A place name can be unusual for no other reason than to reflect thinking of the day. At the opening of the railway station in St Albans Road the road was not named but known as 'the road to St Albans'. A new road was built near the station but not given a name in the accepted term, but called the 'road beyond the station' – a factual description. (It was later named Bedford Street).
A few years later another road was built nearby and this was called 'Back Road', later to be named Church Road.
With 'Water Lane' it can indicate either a lane which went down to the water (river Colne) or that it was a lane down which one went to fetch water. This was something many dwellers would have to do when their water butts were exhausted or wells ran dry. This photograph shows the width of one of the two early lanes leading off the Street, the other being Loates Lane.

Tom Simmonds was born, in 1910, in Whippendell Road but the family soon moved to Water Lane, No. 13. His life, through school days until conscripted into the army where he served until being invalided out in 1944, was centred around Lower High Street

He recalled, 1988, that in his youth he worked at the family business of Simmond's, gentlemens' hairdressers; and at one stage he and his grandfather would go to the cottage hospital, the work-house, and infirmary each morning.

"There we would shave and trim the hair of the inmates. At the workhouse the tramp ward was in the same block and the tramps—hundreds of them—would walk in from either Rickmansworth or St Albans, stay overnight and work next day in the vegetable fields at the back, throughout the day; stay overnight and be on their way early next morning. That was the law."

Of his earlier childhood days Tom recalled that the 'Hill' was an exciting place to live upon. *"Heavily-laden horse-drawn carts would take almost daily loads of export boot polish from the Watford Cobra Works; the horses were thrashed unmercifully to make them gallop up the steep hill. Later, these were replaced by steam driven Foden wagons whose struggles up the hill were accomplished with a shower of hot cinders over the pedestrians."*

The Five Arches Swimming Pool was well used; and the cold water held no terrors. The daily journey to school (Watford Fields) was along the footpath to the river Colne, past Benskin's Malt-House on the left, and Sedgwicks Brewery on the right of the river. Just before meeting with the High Street he would pass a very small sweet factory, where he would always be enticed by the smells, as were swarms of wasps. He crossed the High Street to use Fox Alley and remarked that *"Farthing Lane, (now widened into Watford Fields Road), was then much too dangerous for pedestrians."*

Demolition of the two buildings on the corner of Water Lane, for road widening, revealed the antiquity of the timber-framed structure. Twenty years later, 1974/75, buildings a little further down were due to be demolished for Phase 5 of the road plans, and a minor outcry was caused when it was discovered that they were, in fact, Watford's oldest buildings of which the timbers dated back to the 15th century. Efforts were made to have some of the buildings taken to pieces to be rebuilt elsewhere, but to no avail; they went and few Watfordians mourned their passing.   1952

"The field upon which the College was built frequently flooded and was used by travelling fairs and circuses. The raised footpath used to have the handrail on the inside; if one fell into the roadway that was just too bad!"

As a young boy he spent many happy hours standing on the pathway at the arch end recording the names and numbers of the monster steam engines as they raced their passengers northwards. After leaving school he first worked for the Sun Engraving Printing Works but joined the family firm in 1924. The family by then had moved to Talbot Road, Bushey.

He recalls the anger there was in Watford when the Mansion overlooking the Park was sold and demolished. Every Sunday evening the family used to stroll up the High Street, have an ice-cream in Johnson's Ice Cream Parlour and then stroll to the Park where they would enter the bandstand enclosure and relax listening to the music for a couple of hours.

"After the Mill was burned down there was no need to hold back the water to feed the mill wheel. So the sluice gates were opened and straight way a broad river was reduced to a stream. So there was not enough water in the Five Arches swimming pool to use and we had to go to the new bath near the Town Hall and Library and pay. We used to do our personal shopping at Messrs Oatley's, and Steabben's, both gent's outfitters. These characters grew old, and no-one was prepared to devote their lives to their shops like these characters did. The houses in Water Lane were owned by a Miss Rodwell who lived in a residential house, adjoining the pub, opposite Water Lane. When she died the house was converted into a shop."

Tom came back from the army, and to the shop, shown above, but it was doomed by widening for a ring road scheme, and he left to buy a business in Sidcup in Kent.

The Town Hall, built in 1938 and part-opened in late 1939, had two first-class assembly halls and in years following the war they were used to promote local industry by the holding of Industrial Exhibitions. This, in 1951, was opened by film-star Douglas Fairbanks Jnr. Extremely popular he was considered an "American Ambassador to Great Britain". He is here taking a keen interest in a print-proofing press.

The Coronation was eagerly awaited but in the West Herts Post Mr E J Rogers, of Oxhey, was recounting life in the reign of Elizabeth the First.

"The compulsory Parish Register was a benefit as it made the new Poor Laws possible which could only operate if record of the four million people of the Elizabethan England was kept.

The propaganda plays of Shakespeare reached the plebeian via that form in which he could most easily assimilate it. Today that form is the film. In the country, then, the medium for new ideas would be the priest. The Bible, published in a new language, was made available for all classes by the comparatively new invention of printing. The power of the Lord of the Manor had gone, and by the introduction of the Jury system, Justices of the Peace were instituted by Queen Elizabeth.

One law which benefited master and man alike was the Statute of Artificers (1563) which ensured that every craftsman in town or country had seven years to learn his craft under the eye of a master who was responsible for him in the street as well as in the workshop, and we read in the Act–'Until a man grow into 23 years he for the most part, though not always, is wild without judgement, and not sufficient experience to govern himself.'

He was allowed to marry after 24 years of age after he had served his apprenticeship, and this proved an asset to the community. The Justices of the Peace covered his indentures, and kept a watchful eye on both apprentice and master. Of it Trevelyan writes–'It was the most practical answer made by our ancestors to the ever present problem of technical education and the difficult 'after-school-age."

The Elizabethan system continued until The Industrial Revolution in the 19th century when it showed signs of weakening, and after the first World War it fell apart. The loss has not yet been made good.

A system of Poor Law Relief had to be instituted, and the first workhouse were built. These were a social accomplishment on the part of the state, which alleviated much suffering among the poor. The workhouse was not residential in those days but more of a centre where work was found and distributed when a master was forced to shut up shop."   *W H Post, May 1953*

And on page 82 are comments from Tom Simmonds who tended people who used the workhouse in Watford as late as c1926.

Post-war days were a time of gloom and dismay that shortages and hardships had lasted long after war's end. Consumer goods, in particular, were dreams whetted by adverts promising 'in due course' after export markets were satisfied.

The Coronation of our new Queen, (being 'cried' by our Town Crier outside the Midland Bank in St Albans Road, above), lifted spirits and sent demands soaring for someone who had a television set – few and far between. But, a day or so later the local cinemas would be showing newsreels, in colour, of the spectacle. Locally, tea-parties abounded in schools and halls throughout the Borough with children gaily dressed.

Needless to say, youngsters dressed as portable television sets featured frequently.

This youngster, in Church Road has a dress of empty matchboxes; the reference to strikes as in 'our demands have not been met' was a sign of the times.

This is a mild day in about 1956. Were it bad winter day a good few years earlier all chimneys would be belching their smoke. It is an apt reminder that much of civilisation that we take for granted is far better than hitherto.
St Mary's Road from Church Car Park.

A loan was sanctioned by the Ministry of Health to purchase the Cassio Mill (above, on the Gade, in the park near the lock), and the Council's Estates Committee Chairman directed that 'certain repairs be carried out'. (WHP 31/7/1930). Allowed to rot it was, in 1956, declared a danger area, with gaping holes in the walls and tangled masses of rusted machinery lying in the bottom. A Public appeal was fruitlessly suggested by the Watford Observer.

The better-constructed Grove Mill, 1870, Grove Mill Lane, above, falls outside of Watford, and has been tastefully restored and converted into homes.

Markets are outside affairs; Watford's was no exception, the stalls had awnings to protect their wares and, perhaps, stallholder. On moving from the High Street to its new site the 'open stalls' principle continued, but within the confines of walls and buildings the aisles were narrower and the winter wind more unpleasant. The Market was given a glazed roof by 1932 and was henceforth known as 'the covered Market'.   1956

The Watford Motor Company, opposite Watford Museum, held the agency for Rootes Group products, Humber, Hillman and Singer, Commer and Karrier, and was owned by Benskin's Brewery at the time of opening this showroom in 1957. In 1960 Benskin's proposed to sell the site to R H O Hill's Ltd, who wanted to build on the 12-acre area a large department store, supermarket for food, several medium sized stores, speciality and small shops. The plan was vetoed; the Council could not see it tying in with their road plans, nor did it fit in the Council's own plan for a shopping centre 300 yards up the road, within the relief road scheme. Cawdell's had plans for their site; Clement's were expanding; Gade House was projected. The scheme failed. It is ironical that 39-years later Tesco has all that R H O Hill's wanted.

Carey Place and Lower High Street; all that is greyed-out is either under the Harlequin centre or the Tesco site. The blue swathe is that of the future ring and link roads.

1956

Whole streets and factories would disappear. In the aerial photograph, 1956, above, all that is coloured exists. All that is grey has gone. Clockwise, from the top left hand corner is the erstwhile Sedgwick Brewery. We cross the High Street, at the top, near where the mill once stood and a little way along the street is the entrance to Watford Fields.

In Watford Fields, with Watford Fields Road running between the two playing fields, the mass of Benskins Brewery is on the right hand and in the corner, their new bottling plant being constructed. (Watford Field's School is in the top right corner – the school's playground can be seen).

The railway line cuts across the top quarter of the picture and the area to the left (apart from Water Lane houses) is now the modern Tesco's site. To the right again, Benskin's has been replaced by Watford Springs. Come this side of the railway, below Benskin's. Alongside the railway Norman Reeve's Ford garage has given way, and is under the line of the ring road (here coloured blue). Come along the High Street towards the bottom of the page; stay on the right. You'll recognise the Barclays bank building at King Street, not yet widened, and Burton's and Woolworth's may be seen.

Cross the road at Woolworth's and the white scar is the clearance of the old 'Eight Bells' for a Littlewood's store/Marks & Spencer/Westgate/Primark. Go back along the High Street, crossing Queens Road where you see the Boot's building on the corner. Follow the street along and you pass several old houses, listed, of which the fronts remain. But behind the High Street facade, you see the works, the streets and the houses built mostly built since about 1850/60. Many are here scarcely 100 years old, Clifford street, for example, dating from 1888.

Just a little further and you come to 'Hammond's' corner of Water Lane, where the old cottages can be seen. Just up from the mill, this was the heart of Watford.

It is now an artificial heart, where no one lives; it is Harlequin.

This photograph, 1956, shows Watford's age. At the bottom, a little way up the road, is a light coloured flank wall. It is all that remains of the old Watford Mill, destroyed by fire in 1924 with the remains demolished in 1938. The lower diagonal line from bottom left to the right is the mill stream water course which was once a 'mini-ford' across the earlier road. At top left the framework is erected for Benskin's bottling plant.

The mill-stream's course is easily seen together with the seven-stepped sluice. In the days of the mill the water was always held back to give sufficient head to work the mill. When, after the fire of 1924, the water was lowered, the swimming baths suffered greatly for loss of depth of water.

At the top right of the picture is the entrance to Water Lane. (The pedestrian-crossing across the High Street helps place it.) In the triangle bounded by the High Street, mill stream and Water Lane were the oldest courtyards and houses of Watford. Stapleton's (No. 195) had a 15th century wag-onway and was a 15th century town house.

Before demolition, in 1974, Nos. 177 and 179 were inspected (they were Oatleys menswear shops 70 years previously) and it transpired that parts of the building were also 15th century. Both were older than the almshouses. Borough and County Councils were made aware of this and it was hoped that timbers could be taken and preserved at Chiltern Open Air Museum, but this was not to be. Steabben's across the Street from 177 and 179, also a tailor's shop, proved to have been built in the reign of James I and was over 350 years old.

This length of Street carried the 'Tun Inn' (1600-1740) (Benskin's House site), the 'White Hart' (c1600-1974), the 'Three Crowns' (c1600-1958), 'Leathersellers Arms' (1680-1960), 'Swan' (c1750 - 1997, with modern changes), the 'One Crown' (1750-), 'Brewers Arms' (1839-1911), the 'Fox' (1854-1956), the 'Railway Tavern' (1854-1974), and the 'Rising Sun' (1854-1905).

Many of the buildings, small and compact, and ranged along the street, show their age.

Of this photograph, all that remains are a few cottages in Local Board Road, Watford Field Road, the newer houses at top centre and shops beyond the 'One Crown'. The 'triangle', up to the railway and once containing Watford's oldest history, and many men's allotments, now lies under Tesco's site.

This building, at the corner of Market Place, is shown in the 1832 drawing at the far end of the Market Hall (p13) as of two-storeys. It features again at the end of the crowd in the Market Place, in 1863 (p17), where an additional storey had been added. Here, in 1958, it is due to be demolished to make way for new shops, and is shown afterwards on p101, and, in turn, demolished in 1999.

The 1960s have been labelled 'the Swinging 60s'. The decade had been preceded with plans the public did not understand, and quickly forgot. They wanted shops, and existing shopkeepers wanted more selling space. Gradually the tide turned. The shops fronting the Church went, (to be rebuilt in a 'modern' glass and concrete style), followed by Kinghams (turned into a store for BHS). The 'Spread Eagle', 'Kings Head', 'Green Man', 'Kings Arms' followed the 'Eight Bells' into dust. The bottom of the High Street was changed—a block of four factories was built, but it was still an abject part of town. With new goods flooding the shops, and shops being built to sell them, there was a distinct mood among the younger generations to cock a snook at the hide-bound traditions of their parents and grandparents. They, in the main, 'invented' sex in a way previously unknown.

That there was still great stigma in a child being born out of wedlock, would eventually be a thing of the past. Legalised abortion was coming along, as was the pill. This gave women the freedom to enjoy their lives, and men to take advantage of the fact. But the sky did not fall in, and so was perceived to be in order. The older generations had not the earning capacity of the younger, who thus had the more free spending power. In time came the package holidays; the thrill of flying to sunny beaches and enjoying the nightlife became irresistible.

Cliff Richard's *"We're all going on a summer holiday"* was true for many and aptly captured the mood. In truth, we were enjoying the euphoria which should have been ours at the end of the war, but at that time was denied. Then we were worn-out and broke, and at the mercy of the American pleasure of seeing the British Empire being dismantled. Europe was devastated, America provided aid in abundance. Germany lost the war and won the peace. Rebuilt, their economic revival astonished all. With our very small travel allowance we could not then venture far to see its rebirth. The sixty's dream came true with the availability of cars; people were at last mobile and not at the mercy of buses and trains. Unused rail sidings and branch lines were taken up. Lorries' restrictive speed limits went and road transport, once used at each end of rail links, could take on the entire journey.

We were catching up with Europe and their vast network of motorways and autobahns.

These shops, some listed, fronted Carey Place; some with a history of two to three centuries. For the Harlequin Centre, from Fantos to Boots' corner were rebuilt; Greys (old Chater's, chemists) had the front retained; 133/135, Keith Royle, is retained as is 137, Crown Wallpapers, on the corner of Carey Place; 139 and 141 have mock fronts; 143/145, Mac Fisheries is retained in style if not in actuality. Bratt's 147, is rebuilt and 149/151 (Maynard Jewellers and Lavells, confectioners) retained or rebuilt similar.   *1960*

     That Watford's one road was not really suitable for this era was another matter. Buses and delivery vehicles (whether direct from supplier or from the Junction goods yard) clogged the High Street. The 'Street' groaned and a plan was put into operation to carve a short relief road from Market Street to Upton Road, where traffic could rejoin.

     This was tinkering. It gave the Street a 'pedestrian precinct' (which it never really became) and allowed traffic to flow from Queens Road to Market Street in one direction only, thus making a 'race track'. It was realised that this was a stop-gap, and further plans introduced, to be carried out in eight phases. The phases started slowly. Involved was the building of Charter place; changes to Vicarage/Wiggenhall Road junction; Town Hall flyover/underpass; Eastern Relief Road (Beechen Grove); Mars Site; West Watford Link; Dual carriageway in Clarendon Road and redevelopment of Nascot for residential use with some shops.

     The work took place over a long time—never-ending it seemed, and with mistakes—it gave us a ring road, designed for an anti-clockwise traffic flow, and for pedestrians, much-hated underpasses. It also took from us, in 1970, a prized possession of the town, the Park Gates, to widen Rickmansworth Road in preparation for the Town Hall underpass constructed in 1971.

     In the meantime the horrible little bridge in Balmoral Road was being rebuilt to take two-way traffic, it had been complained of since the 1930s (although Balmoral Road to Radlett Road had been made up). The tunnel under the railway bridge at the end of Water Lane now had a pedestrian walkway, and traffic lights to control the vehicles, and there was talk in the air about steam engines being phased out, as electrification came into being. If that happened Watford's most detested black spot, the St Albans Road bridge over the railway, would go into oblivion.

     In 1954 the bridge carried a daily an average of 882 vehicles per hour, plus 165 pedal cycles; in the rush hour this increased to 1,211 vehicles and 1,452 cycles. The High Street in the Market Place averaged 697 vph and 224 cycles and 935 vph at peak times plus 480 cycles. Similar figures were recorded for Rickmansworth and Hempstead Road.

It wasn't known at the time of taking this photograph that within two to three years the landscape would permanently alter and Henry Kingham's (three-storied white building on the right) would give way to British Home Stores and that, later, Cawdell's would also disappear. 1960

The Odeon by the Pond, high Street, Watford. Closed 1963, demolished 1964. Pond, 2003

The newspaper office, 101 High Street, corner of Loates Lane, was centrally placed to observe and report the news, and, at its side, the original printer's business to execute private and business printing. The news and gossip photographs on display were much admired. Occupied by C H Peacock Ltd since about 1897 the shops are in their last year, before being demolished in 1961. The 'Observer' continued in Loates Lane, then Rickmansworth Road and, now, Caxton Way, in an electronic era.

Watford's first recording medium, though not then seen as such, was the Parish Register, started in 1539. Dates of births, marriages and deaths were sometimes interspersed with details of the lives and times of the parishioners, and as such were much trawled over by earlier writers, notably Henry Williams c1880 and W R Saunders c1919-20 (their valuable extracts time and time again re-used!). Both used their researches in published histories of which the latter's 'History of Watford' (1931) was the most informative. The Registers are now in the care of Hertford's Record Office.

The 'Watford Observer' was started in 1863, in Queen Street; the 'Watford and West Herts Post' at 42 High Street in 1887, taking over in 1919 the 'Watford Newsletter' (1908 to 1919) printed in King Street. Mr C H Peacock acquired in 1896 the 'Herts Leader' and shop at the corner of Loates Lane where the 'Observer' was henceforth to be printed. The 'West Herts Post' was first printed at 42 High Street, then in Carey Place, then, with offices near the Pond, at Luton.

Thomson's Regional Newspapers introduced the 'Evening Echo' in 1967 and the introduction led to the closing of the 'Post' in May 1970—at about the time the Park Gates went—so thus Watford lost two favoured landmarks. The 'Evening Echo' lasted until 1983 when it, too, folded.

Subsequently Watford was covered by the 'Review', a St Albans-based free-sheet. In later years the 'Watford Observer' and C H Peacock Ltd were absorbed into Westminster Press who in turn were absorbed into the Newsquest Media Group and who in 1999 further absorbed the 'Review'.

The 'West Herts Post' had been much appreciated, it being the first to employ its own photographers and use photographs extensively; it had a 'common-touch' which sometimes better gauged the feelings of its readers. It championed the causes of the 'common-man' more loudly than did the 'Observer', but made a big mistake when, in the late twenties, it saw no need for the Public Baths (in Hempstead Road). During the postwar years of development plans it joined with the 'Observer' on matters of importance and thus presented to the Council a united front which was hard to ignore.

Now, for the first time in 112 years, Watford has only one newspaper albeit offering one paid and two free versions, the 'Observer', 'Free Observer' and in some areas the 'Review.

The traffic jam on Whitsun Carnival day of 1960 just seemed worse, with some drivers sitting reading! The wooded ground is that of 'Woodlands' which gave its name to the block of shops erected in 1963.

Alderman Thomas F Harris, J P, Mayor of Watford, presenting the Scroll conferring Freedom of Entry to the Borough of Watford to Lt General Sir Reginald Denning KBE, CB, of the 3rd East Anglian Regiment in July 1959. This grants the privilege of marching through the Borough of Watford, on ceremonial occasions, with colours flying, bands playing, drums beating and bayonets fixed.

This privilege was exercised in 1962 upon the return of the regiment from a tour of duty in Singapore and to mark the change of name to 'Royal Anglian Regiment'; the presenting Mayor was then Alderman J R Hicks.

The Town Hall roundabout looking along Rickmansworth Road on a Whitsun Carnival day. The police presence looked as if they were in control, but were not. The Super is in the distance walking back from the park having gained a first hand sighting. There were, in 1960, no mobile phones!

With the crowds in the park it is difficult to guess the reason for the glum look. His horses, at least, suffered neither heat nor traffic jam!
1960

There are five eras represented by various shops in this 1960's picture of Lower High Street almost opposite the Museum. The first was Swann's – a hundred years earlier, that of Watford's first police station. Into a different era it heralded the town's early business life as a saddler's and leather goods merchant.

The third era was that of the fish and chip shop – a staple convenience diet of pre-war years, The fourth is of Stapleton's, an early specialist serving the motor trade with tyres and batteries.

The fifth is the run-down state of the second-hand clothes shop. In 1965 there were few years of life left before a further phase of roadworks would see the lot pulled down.

Below: An early plan for the eastern relief road. It will be noted that there is no flyover, but an access road from the High Street into a roundabout in Clarendon Road.

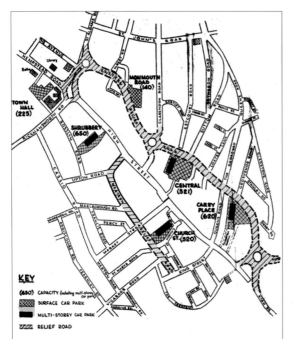

To make a relief road meant that the Borough Engineer and his staff faced huge difficulties.

Mr Sage used imaginative ideas to meet them; he knew that many houses and buildings would have to go for the good of the community and the motorist in particular, and did not shrink from facing harsh decisions.

Another problem had to be faced; Hemel Hempstead was a 'new town' and was going to build a modern shopping centre along Marlowes and it was feared that Hemel would take trade from Watford. This, of course would not do, for had not Watford, for the past 100 years, seen itself as the pre-eminent shopping centre for many miles around?

His plan, in January, to make a relief road, carving much property out of Clarendon Road, showed an insensitivity which angered many business men. An alternative was soon found. A flyover.

Queens Road in a quiet and peaceful mood. The oft-made statement that 'there's not much traffic about' is because many street photographs were taken on either a Wednesday afternoon, when shops were closed for the afternoon. or on a Sunday. Then, without shoppers and traffic, the buildings could be seen. In the distance the Wesleyan Church on the corner of Beechen Grove/Queens Road. 1960. Inset 2003.

The plans that were envisaged were endorsed by County, but would of necessity have to wait many years before leases fell in and properties become available; it was an impossibility to purchase compulsorily the amount of land needed.

The blight imposed was gradual, but, nevertheless started.

It added to the general run-down appearance of the Lower High Street and, later, Queens Road. It was recognised that the relief road scheme could not progress quickly, but something still needed to be done. And quickly. A resurrected 1959 'one-way' plan had merit that it was cheap to implement –merely many signs and gallons of paint. It made Lower High Street one-way; blocked off the High Street at Market Place and created a mini-race-track.

A few day's blizzard was followed by a quick thaw and the traditional flood areas of Lower High Street and Wiggenhall Road were inundated. Wiggenhall Road's new industrial estate had been expecting the floods. Precautions were taken but the flood, in December 1960, was more severe than expected and the damage considerable. The flooded field on the right, scene of many fairs, was later host to Stephenson College, on stilts, now the petrol station of Tesco.   Inset, 2001

Lower High Street Gas Works coking plant in the same 1960 flood. At that time Holland and Norway were enjoying North Sea gas (then too far to be piped to the UK). Newer gasfields allowed us to benefit in 1971.

Dr Tibble's Vi-Cocoa factory was started at Bushey Mill Lane/Sandown Road in 1899; and three years later suffered a disastrous fire. As the 'Watford Manufacturing Company' they masterminded local munitions productions in the Great War. They expected great business thereafter, and had this factory built. It was a white elephant which bankrupted the company and remained empty until taken by British Moulded Hose (and who used the top floor during WWII for producing Penicillin). This fire in June 1961 gutted much of the building, but was later restored. BMH relinquished the site in 1977 and the building was demolished. See p55.

A 'fire engine' was authorised to be purchased in 1600 to augment the 'firehooks' (used to pull down burning walls) and leather buckets. A Vestry entry in 1747 gives details of £68 being sanctioned for two engines and their appurtenances. The village did not need, then, much more. The 'engines' were merely small hand-pulled carts which held a container into which water would be poured, from a relay of buckets; it would then be pumped through a short hose, by means of a hand pump worked by two men, one each side of the appliance. It was entirely suitable for fighting small fires in the cottages.

A Volunteer Fire Brigade was formed in 1867; in the year after, it purchased its first engine, 'Vesta', horse-drawn, the pump manually operated. Sedgwick's, a year later, established their own brigade and henceforth always co-operated in fighting local fires. Sedgwick's horse-drawn steamer was purchased in 1876, Watford's in 1900.

The Volunteers' early engine house was at 116 High Street, This became inadequate and a new station built at 14 High Street, opened in 1900. The now Fire and Ambulance service moved to Rickmansworth Road, on the Cassiobury Farm site, in February 1961.

A 1747 hand-drawn Vestry 'Engine' shown in Albert St, near Carey Place, c1925

The Fire Station c1956; to its left No. 14 High, the old Urban District Offices, here let to small commercial firms and as a general-purpose meeting place. In 1938, with about 80 fire and 2000 ambulances calls a year a new station was needed. Nascot Road was chosen of three sites and a prize of £150 awarded to the winning design. War intervened and the fire station stayed put. Inset, corner of Gade House, 2004.

Below: the Montague Burton Group joined forces with the Co-op to develop this site at a reputed cost of £½m. The old Council Offices have been demolished leaving only air-raid shelters standing. When rebuilt as Gade House delivery access to rear of the shops was poor, in particular blocking services to Woodlands Parade shops and offices.

Offered to the Urban District Council they did not take the opportunity to clear the decrepit shops in front of the Church. The Council bought piecemeal, from 1930, but in 1961 demolished the old and rebuilt in glass and concrete. The upper floors were to the street line, the ground floor being set back to give a wider pavement. The clearing in 1999 enabled St Mary's Square to be built. The earlier vista is on page 90.

The corner of Church Street and New Street; the three-storey building to the left was once Watford's workhouse before new premises in Vicarage Road (Union House). All is under Church Car Park (inset).   1960.

The Railway Cottages, alongside St Albans Road railway bridge (below), looking splendid but empty, were in the line of the projected dual carriageway. The spot is now approximately Homebase car park.   1961

St Albans Road railway bridge was the worst of Hertfordshire's five bad-road black spots. (Watford High Street was second). In a rush hour, back in 1954, 1,211 vehicles, of which 110 were buses, and 1,452 pedal cycles would pass. An average hour saw 882 vehicles and 165 bicycles pass. In 1935 a week's census counted 24,105 cyclists – 3,443 daily. The bridge was rebuilt as dual carriageway in late 1961; the railway's electrification followed in two phases, April 1966 and March 1967

Henry Kingham's grocery business started in the High Street opposite the Church in a house turned shop. It expanded into a well-respected retail and wholesale grocer's. But the wholesale trade could not adequately be served from its town location and when Greenhill Crescent was laid out, a new large office and warehouse distribution centre was built for Kingham's. It is now Park House, subdivided into units.   1962

That Cassiobury Park Gates and Lodge were not hugely old did not matter. Plans to demolish were mooted in 1967 and then many older residents would have had memories of the fight to have the park, and of the successful outcome in 1909. Entering the park through the Gates was something special. Today's field-like entrance does little justice to the natural beauties of the park.   1967

From nightfall of New Year's Eve 1961 (a Sunday) the snow fell incessantly until about four a.m. New Year's Day was not, then, a holiday and the Corporation's snow ploughs were out from 5am, but the normally busy Monday saw a deserted town as few braved the journey to work.

Right; the parked mini belonged to one worker who made the effort.

The semi-frozen pond, street lights and pond's concealed lighting present a fairyland view.

The Gates in a picture postcard setting, January 1st 1962.

It did not takes the town's youngsters long to ignore the beauty of nature and take advantage of the opportunity for fun and sport which had miraculously appeared.
The hill is of the West Herts Golf Course just beyond the bridge and canal in the park.

Many of the town's photographers enjoyed the rare spectacle of trees wreathed in a mantle of snow, and caressed with the warm light of a wintry sun.

The shoppers cursed, slipping and sliding along the pavements upon which, in parts along the Parade, the snow had been shovelled and banked to some three feet high, leaving only a narrow walkway.

"Let us not be surrounded by a tarmac girdle."

Town Clerk, December 1953

The 22-year forecast for Watford included 6,400 houses, 12 schools, 100 new shops (including 40 at Cow-lane and Sewage Farm), 100 acres of industrial sites (Cassiobridge Sewage Farm and Station Estate), a new police station, telephone exchange, extension to the gas works; much of which was scheduled for before 1958. New roads included the Birmingham Radial (M1, 1956) Road improvements were suggested for Radlett Road and Horseshoe Lane. Also included was a line for the Aylesbury Radial Road.

On the diagram that in light-brown came to pass; that in grey did not.

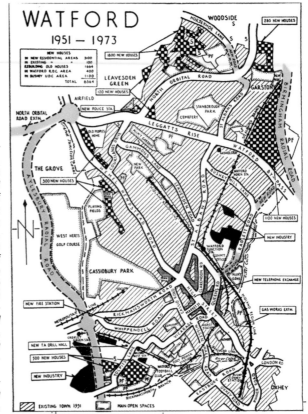

In February 1952 Watford gained a new Town Clerk, Gordon H Hall, and one of the first items to cross his desk would have been the outline plan for the future of the town. They were far reaching in the scope of expansion. Traffic was then relatively light but included thousands of cyclists.

The M1 (Birmingham Radial) was planned prior to 1939 but not yet built.

Neither the then new Borough Engineer or the Town Clerk had deep working knowledge of Watford and, of course, could not foresee the future, especially the M1 in 1959.

The Aylesbury Road skirted the West Herts Golf Course and at the Inquiry in December 1953 the Town Clerk instanced that 'within a few hundred yards was the entrance to the park where Watfordians and others could walk for miles without thinking they were near an urban area.'

He produced a Sealed Deed relating to the purchase [of the park] which stated that the open space should be maintained by the Corporation as an open space 'for public use forever'.

Mr Sage suggested an alternative that would go west of Whippendell Woods from Rousebarn Farm and join the western extension of North Orbital Road [M25] "which would be constructed in any case" about a half mile west of the junction proposed by the Ministry. This alternative, he claimed, would cost no more and be only half a mile longer.

This suggestion seems not have been taken up and in the course of time the plans and proposals seemed forgotten. But–the housing, schools, industry and shop took place as did the M1. The opening of the M1 drew hauliers from Slough and the west and for many years the journey through the Denham Bypass, Mill End, Rickmansworth, Croxley, Rickmansworth Road, the Town Hall Rounbabout came to grinding halt at the St Albans Road bottle-neck of the narrow railway bridge.

In December 1958 the Minister of Housing, Mr Henry Brooke, deleted the project saying, **"although there is evidence of need for the section of this road between Pinner and Hunton Bridge, the amount of traffic that would use it is uncertain, and much would depend on the other road proposals yet to be carried out. In view of the serious effect**

A noose is put in place around the town centre.

May 20th, 1962

Above, the day that the High Street ceased being a through-road.
Left; Hempstead Road tail-back past the Library and Horns pub. Rickmansworth Road was then, and still is, the only access way to Croxley.

of this proposal on Whippendell Woods and the golf course at Watford he has, therefore, deleted the section between Cassio Bridge and the proposed North Oribital Road near Hunton Bridge."

In the meantime Mr Sage concentrated upon speeding traffic through the High Street by blocking it and introducing a mini ring-road, designed to eventually have the traffic flow reversed to gain better access to bus stops and car parks. **That part of the plan failed,** and Watford has an inner 'tarmac girdle' which, until 2004, has obliged pedestrians to use underpasses.

The flow of traffic, held up by the cross flow at the roundabout needed attention. At first a flyover was suggested, but being adjacent to the Town Hall was converted into an underpass. In the road widenings necessary for this and the Eastern relief road (from Town Hall/St Albans Road to Clarendon Road) much property was lost, including the Park Gates which the Town Clerk had been advised were "of no historical importance."

The 1962 plan achieved little apart from eliminating the bottle necks of King Street/Queens Road interchange. Black dots along some roads indicate car parking.

After 1962's alterations there was less traffic in the High Street, but traffic crept back with delivery transport prominent for the smaller shops. Charter Place, with extensive underground space mean that deliveries to larger stores were off-road. Towards the end of the 1900's a tide of 'orange-badge' holders, most genuine, parked along both sides of the precinct. Pedestrians were again confined to narrow pavements.

Collier's on the corner of Clarendon Road and High Street when 'window shopping' was still possible with store windows well-lighted along the shopping centre.

Watford Junction Station, an evening rush hour in 1977, gave no indication of the massive changes which were just 'down the line'. The old station booking office and forecourt went in 1985 and a new station built (1986) which included a multi-storey office complex above. The small freight yard in Woodford Road now serves as a 'mini' bus station'.
Inset; Station Road and Junction Station, 2004

At the station a prospective traveller in July 1982 faces the fact that an ASLEF strike had brought the system to a standstill.

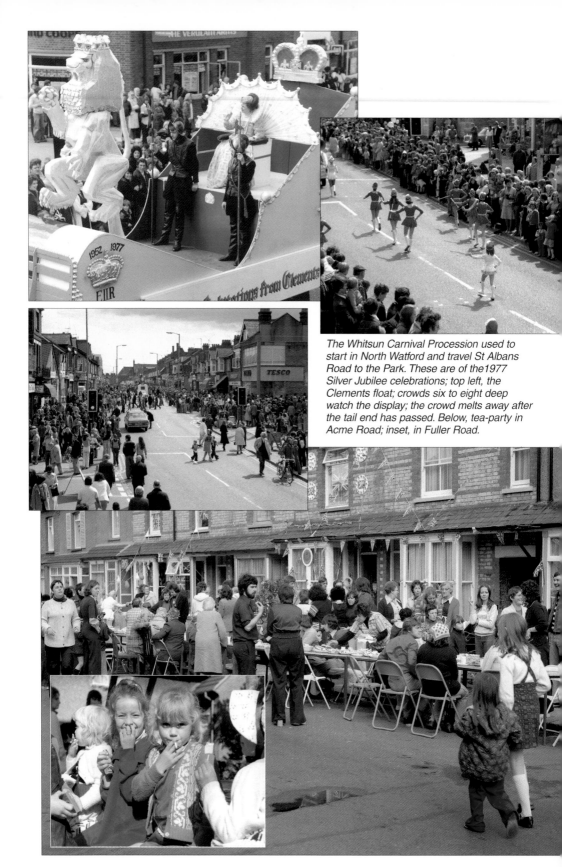

The Whitsun Carnival Procession used to start in North Watford and travel St Albans Road to the Park. These are of the 1977 Silver Jubilee celebrations; top left, the Clements float; crowds six to eight deep watch the display; the crowd melts away after the tail end has passed. Below, tea-party in Acme Road; inset, in Fuller Road.

The Carlton Cinema in Clarendon Road closed in 1980 and was used for a time as a carpet warehouse before demolition and an office block built in its stead. Part of the new block houses the 'Green Room' of the Palace Theatre, itself finishing a two-year refit in 2004.

The Odeon (1937 Gaumont) closed in 1983. The Council had taken the 'courageous' decision of buying the many and various interests in the site, and the ground behind, which Tesco turned down, to be taken up by Sainsbury's. This enabled Sainsbury's to move from their temporary site (Tech School site) in Queens Road thus allowing the Harlequin project to start. Here, shops and snooker hall were provided.　　　*1983*

Albert Fishburn was an ink technician of American Ault & Wiborg; called up when the US entered the war he served in England in 1918. Upon demob he stayed in England and in 1929 he, with Lt Col the Hon Bertram Russell, founded Fishburn Printing Ink Co Ltd, at Cassiobury Mills. At that time there were printed nearby waxed discs for milk bottle tops – for which Fishburn's gained a contract to make the specialised ink. Packaging of food products, especially breadwrapping, cellulose wrappings (and later, polythene), corrugated cardboard cartons, all needed new inks of types and characteristics not previously made.

Tin printing needed new inks (and during WWII, inks which had to act as a preservative layer to cans 'untinned'). Colour printing, prewar, was not common – but the art of direct-lithography for printing posters was highly developed and also needed special inks which had resistance to fading and industrial corrosion. Fishburn's pioneered many innovations in printing inks. Control passed to the Inmont Corporation of America, retaining the 'Fishburn' name. 'Fishburn's' was acquired by BASF in 1986 and finally vacated the site in 1990. Cassiobury Mills demolished is now 'Homebase'.

Firemen from local forces combine to fight a warehouse blaze at Keuhne & Nagel's premises in Colonial Way, in 1989, when damage estimated at £8,000,000 was caused. Two years later a blaze at Pickford's storage depot, near Colonial Way, destroyed household contents including irreplaceable personal possession. This was later followed by a blaze which destroyed Knutsford School, and in May 2004 one which destroyed Bradford Wing of Shrodell's Hospital, fortunately used only for storage.

The 'Peace' in Rickmansworth Road, 1985 had been closed for some while with some windows boarded. A little later the side wings and buildings to the rear were demolished and cleared, only the centre block remaining. That it remained unused with an undetermined future caused resentment, especially when the clock was taken in broad daylight. Local opinion was later satisfied when the building was refurbished and opened in 1996 as the 'Peace Hospice'.

Kett's on the corner of Queens Road had occupied the site following Boot's moving into their new store on the Rose and Crown Hotel site at the corner of Market Street. A little way along Queens Road are the ex-premises of Sainsbury's, Watfords first fair-sized supermarket, with a car park adjacent. Woolworth's building, overhanging on the left, was closed in January 1990, and rebuilt as a small parade of shops.

Greville's Studios, on the corner of Queens Road and Beechen Grove was Watford's first purpose-built Post and Sorting Office. Here it is in the direct line of road widening to suffer the same fate as the handful of streets on the other side of the road, around and including Carey Place. Allied Carpets on the right was once the Wesleyan Church, and is now in 2004 pulled down to become a large block of apartments. The cars are queueing to enter 'Clifford Street' car park.

Albert Road, Charles Street, Derby Road and part of Clifford Street had been cleared; the space thus cleared became the car park nearest to the rear entrance of Sainsbury's. Flank wall in the distance carries the name Hudson & Stracey – a reminder of the several print works of the area.

The Endowed Schools in Derby Road were opened in 1884. The hole in the foreground (part of Harlequin foundations) was cut in the autumn of 1988; the chalk was once sea-bed 70-90 million old. In more recent times the ground above was once home to Carey Place factories. Underneath the centre is a labyrinth of vehicle loading bays, many capable of taking the largest articulated vehicles to service some of the stores.

Queens Road has the south side construction work rapidly progressing. The works were a natural barrier to shoppers not bothering to go further down the High Street. Posters proclaimed "There is life further down" and listed some of the shops. Trewins continued trading from their Queens Road premises.

Above; M1 Link Road. The Watford
By-Pass was completed in 1926. Two
years later suggestions were
made for a link into Lower High
Street. It came about in 1991 just in
time to serve Harlequin! This bridge
under construction is across the
Colne near Water Lane road bridge.

Below; May 1992 saw the craning out
of Phase Three shuttering and scaf-
folding no longer needed. The crane
was one of Baldwin's largest with a jib
length of 90m (295ft). On the corner
of Queens Road and High Street is
the Nat-West Bank, soon to be closed
and demolished.

The montage showing the food court area in 1994. In the past months (early 2004) the food units were closed and the area cleared and part has been turned into another store. 'Atlas', long ceased revolving, has gone; the escalators remain.

Above; Christmas atmosphere 2002 and, right, a visiting Salvation Army Band plays popular carols.

When it was realised that a water facility could not, after all, be provided in a shopping complex the Benskin's site seemed a good alternative. Built in a great rush to avoid restrictions by the Government upon spending the project was flawed from the start. Opened in November 1990 the Council were proud to state that the project cost "the Council only 12% more than it would cost taxpayers to build just one mile of the M25 motorway." The finished cost was estimated at £10,000,000. In 1997 the Springs were closed from summer to October for essential works. In August 2000 it was announced that major structural faults would need a large investment to correct. Watford Council were advised that 'in order to keep the Springs open for the next few years would require an investment of £8,000,000' and stated that residents could not be expected to pay as only 35% of those using the Springs were Watford Council residents; the remaining 65% were from outside the Borough. But those from 'outside' did shop locally whilst other members of their family, etc, enjoyed the Springs. Watford Springs closed in December and was demolished in 2001.

The design and building of 'Mars 1', ('The Harlequin Centre'), was to be a saga of political strife as factions wanted promises kept. Throughout most plans for increasing the shopping centres within Watford were inducements such as 'flats', 'amenity areas', 'dance halls' and 'billiard halls'. Harlequin was promised with swimming facilities and when part of the Council found out that they were not, after all, to be included in final plans, there was an outcry. The builders could see no way of including in a shopping mall an appropriate-sized swimming and bathing facility. Deals were done; housing which should have been built upon the Benskin's Brewery site was re-planned for Tolpits Lane (Isolation Hospital site), and the 'Watford Springs' leisure complex hurriedly planned and built.

The baths saga had started with the urban District Council suggesting, in January 1899, that Watford needed proper baths. No action was taken. At the end of the Great war, 1918, the Watford Manufacturing Co Ltd—one of the largest manufacturers in the town, and with an exemplary record of cleanliness in their food manufacturing plant, re-opened the 'baths' question.

At the beginning of the century better class houses had bathrooms with a gas geyser, others had a coal-fired boiler for heating water for boiling and washing clothes; for personal washing a stand-up rinse would suffice, or a large tin tub used. Some more recent houses equipped with a bathroom drew the hot water from the boiler. This would have sufficed for most dwellers, but for troops and war workers billeted on the many older homes, the lack of bath facilities was keenly felt.

Nothing was done until the question was re-opened in 1929, and 24 baths, 12 for each sex proposed, quickly drawing comments that that was not sufficient. Many petitions were presented, 500 women residents on one, and another from women from the Co-op Guild from Harebreaks, and a scheme costing £33,000 projected. In October of 1931 work started at the rear of the Elms site. Slipper baths for both sexes were provided as well a first-class swimming pool.

When finished and opened in May of 1933 they were believed to be the first electrically heated baths in the world, the Borough Engineer, Mr Newman being responsible for design and carrying out the scheme. Opening the baths, the Mayor, Alderman J Evans, said that the baths "were an example of how Watford was living up to the times". It was soon decided to permit mixed bathing although Cllr H Horwood thought that some men might be shy of going in with the ladies.

Watford Springs, conceived of political arguments and dogma, was an exciting project but, sadly, doomed to disappointing failure.

Reflected in Harlequin's glass is the image of Barclay's Bank on the corner of King Street, closed in 1998. The Harlequin work started in December 1988; Queens Road shops were finally closed and pulled down as were the shops fronting the High Street. Some were listed buildings and of these the rear parts went and the front facades left. The fronts were strengthened and new rears grafted on or incorporated into the new structure. No. 147 serves as an entrance. The first phase, which included W H Smith, Boots, Trewins, Gas and Electricity showrooms opened in August 1990. The second phase in 1991 and the final third in June 1992. All were on time. The third phase extended to link with Charter Place and, through Marks and Spencer's to the High Street.

A youngster looking in Halford's shop on the Parade. Not long after, Halford's joined the exodus to leave the High Street and entered the realm of retail units at the Lower High Street near Bushey Arches.

The Beacon

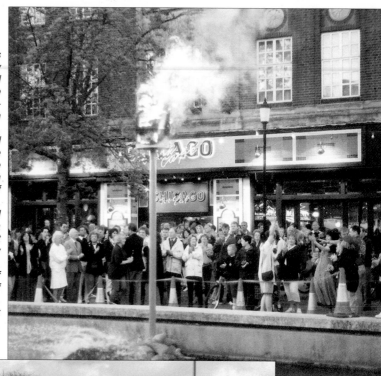

To celebrate 50 years since V-day (Victory in Europe) a national Day of Remembrance was held with a two-minute silence on May 8th 1995. A maroon was fired from the top of the YMCA building and the sound at 8.38pm heralded the start of the Silence. This was followed by the lighting of a symbolic beacon – part of a national chain – by Mayor Maria Green. Representatives of Watford's twin towns of Nanterre, Pesaro, Novgorod and Mainz participated.

Where were the Park Gates?
Near the entrance to Cassiobury Park from Rickmansworth Road two of the park paths converge; they point to the gate position. It would have been approximately on this stretch of road a little in front of the two cars.

Widening the road took from the Peace Hospital a large part of their front grounds for which the Bromet Statuary Group had to be removed, to the library precinct. The left-hand figure is dedicated to the fallen, never to return; the right hand to the maimed, especially the blind for he is depicted as groping; the centre, waving his hand, expresses victory 'we have won'.

Whitsun changed to Spring Bank Holiday and the Bank Holiday Monday was a fun day out for the family; the horse show drew entries from far around and in the afternoon and evening the fun fair.

It was too good to last. The organisers needed more space than the park could provide. For the carnival procession the source of vehicles for the old-style floats dried.

The activities in the park evolved into an 'environment fair', then plus a music day and then into the Rainbow Festival.

The latter, in 2003 was so extraordinarily successful that Health and Safety said to calm it; there were too many people and too few toilet and similar facilities. These pictures 1995.

Here for the beer

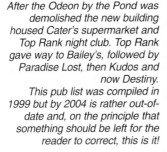

After the Odeon by the Pond was demolished the new building housed Cater's supermarket and Top Rank night club. Top Rank gave way to Bailey's, followed by Paradise Lost, then Kudos and now Destiny.
This pub list was compiled in 1999 but by 2004 is rather out-of-date and, on the principle that something should be left for the reader to correct, this is it!

Any Watfordian, returning after an absence of a few years, may wonder what has overtaken the top end of the Street. Once a rather grand Parade (of shops) the ring road system and flyover did it no favour and, as if to hide the damage, the remains were smothered with fast-growing trees.

In 1998 the Council realised that foliage and shrub beds planted on the top of the old road were not, after all, quite so good. Women had been disinclined to use the road during the long nights of the darker half of the year. The decorative lanterns and black shop windows cast little light and caution was deemed prudent. After the exodus to Harlequin, led from the top by Moselle's, many large High Street shops became empty shells. The knock-on effect forced others to close or move out of Watford thus increasing the depressingly large stock of empty premises.

The Council, c1990, thought a cafe quarter would be a good idea and over the past ten years many large premises have been turned into pubs/theme bars/clubs totalling some fourteen (1999):
They are, from Market Place to St Albans Road:

'Old Westminster' was	Provincial/NatWest Bank
'Rat & Parrot'	Dixon's (Buck old premises)
'Moon Under Water'	Grange Furnishing (Watford) Ltd
'Pancho's Villa'	Dunn's Hatters/Outfitter's
'O'Neills'	Halford's/FineFare/(extending into Beatties)
'Ice-O-Bar'	FineFare
'Bar Risa' & 'Jongleurs'	FineFare
'Hogwash'	Peter Spivey
'Yates'	Chef Corner/Walter Gasson
'Artichoke'	Cakebread Robey/Oliver
'Destiny'	Plaza/Odeon Cinema/Kudos
'Chicago Rock Cafe'	Electricity Showrooms
'Scruffy Murphy's'	Westminster Bank

'Destiny' and 'Jongleurs' are night clubs

Gade House has yet to be redeveloped, but will be another 'leisure/theme pub' activity.

In addition about fifteen shops have been turned into cafes, sandwich bars or take-aways—the latter serving mainly the vibrant night life. This concentration of night-life has worried residents of the

The 1930's Wheatsheaf was built further back from the old to allow for road widening. It was demolished in 1994 to be replaced by Tempo Electrical Warehouse, in turn to be replaced by a Mercedes Dealership, (inset).

Baraka, right, occupies part of Gade House.

locality who have voiced fears of disturbances and violence, but are ignored.

From time to time window repairers board up broken windows; shop-keepers wash down their pavements early in mornings, local residents look ruefully at more damage done to their parked cars and council workmen re-correct signs turned the wrong way. It is no comfort to be told that none of this damage is 'wilful or malicious' but just 2am boisterous high spirits.

One hundred years ago, 1899, the Urban District Council invested in electricity and they liked the boom in prosperity that it sparked. They embarked upon a campaign of 'selling' the town; a trait which has continued ever since. The available land has been sold, and built upon; much land is now being recycled. Where once was a large house and garden now becomes several blocks of 'town houses'. The effect upon congestion is insidious and cumulative.

The blocks of offices in Clarendon Road were designed to attract workers into Watford. For each who commutes in there are those who who commute out. The effect upon congestion is apparent. A 'Green Bus Route' is laid upon North Watford with the designed effect of harassing drivers to use the buses. The buses have never, ever, been able to provide the standard of service needed by a community. Mobility is essential and car owners must get to work, they use back roads; which become clogged. The congestion started long ago when the Market Place was turned into a car park in 1928.

In self-defence, groups throughout the town have formed Residents' Associations to offer a check to mistakes in planning details which escape Town Hall officials, and to campaign to keep their environmental standards from slipping because of overdevelopment. A notable introduction was the 1998 Controlled Zone Parking Scheme, throughout central Watford, which removed the blight of residents, especially near the Junction, being unable park near their homes. The Central Association has had a hard and long fight to curb the excesses from town centre late-night binge drinking. But, to keep tabs upon the town centre populace some 29 CCTV cameras are monitored 24 x 7 x 365days.

Each year.

Above: A mask, one of the eight from St Mary's Square

Right: the Memory Wall near the Town Hall.

Above: The Hornet, opposite Queens Road is by Heather Burrell; the Sensory Garden Spiral by Andrew Moakes; The Memory Wall by Carl Fielscher
Café Nero, next to the Square, gives a Continental air.

The town centre art, 1998-2000, was largely funded by an Arts Lottery Grant worth £96,000.

The St Mary's Square art, by Philip Bews and Diane Gorvin, of four 5-metre-high stainless steel tripods, carry masks representing the themes of friendship or an aspect of Watford. The bases link features of our twin towns.

Leavesden aerodrome, early 1970's.
1. The A405 before dualling. 2. Courtlands Drive/A41 crossing. 3. No. 1 Flight Shed (Mosquito/Halifax)
4. M1 spur to Maple Cross. 5. No. 1 Factory, LAP Group, now Leavesden Studios. 6. South Way
7. Langleybury Church. 8. 1000yd runway. 9. Hunters Lane. 10. No 2 Factory, de Havilland Aircraft Co.
11. Leavesden High Road

*Right; Leavesden Film Studios upon the
site of the No. 1 factory.
Below; a park of high-tech offices upon
the site of de Havilland/Rolls Royce No. 2
factory. The nearby estate of new housing
have street names which perpetuate
aircraft and aircraft industry names and
people.*

Time, work, emigration and immigration . . .

They, the early flint-using men, had no means of counting the passing of days. Perhaps one of the group was more thoughtful than the others and had a prized piece of bone upon which he carved a log of the days, or summers, which had passed since they had started their wanderings. His period of time would have no reference except his, and his mate's, lifetime. The great stone circles, later, were a time-marking machine for designers and builders who knew the how and why. For Christians a birth 2,000 years ago acts as marker but even in Henry VIII's time events were reckoned as '37the year of King Henry VIII's reign' much as was done in the times of the Egyptian Pharaohs.

Wandering is, as we have seen, an old established trait. It is fostered by a need to better oneself for either the need to live—food and work—or for a better climate or environment. It is the desire to maintain life which drives most people to move.

In the 1950s, days of depression and shortages and stifling restrictions, a considerable number of this country's younger people decided to emigrate. A main reason was stated as 'to give our children a better chance'. Their choice, for they then saw little future in their homeland.

From the late 1800s, within a century, the population had gradually moved from abject serfdom and excruciatingly hard working conditions into a more civilised era. This was hard won, largely by union power which fought for shorter hours and better wages, and by suffragettes who wanted, not equality, but better rights for women. Levering a population into better standards was long and hard, and when the standards had risen many unions wanted still more. Not for nothing was Watford known as the second richest town in the county—based on the biggest printers' wages. But high wages out of proportion make costs higher, and heavier to bear for those not so privileged.

Wealth does not so easily spread.

Affordability and mobility in the form of the car enables many to travel further to places of employment; no longer were workers tied to a factory within walking distance or a cycle ride away, and so employers' domination gradually relaxed. Workers had choice.

Pace of progress has been immense; methods of electronic communication mean that much work can be achieved swiftly and with less labour; and the end result is the greatest disaster of all in that machine and computer has reduced the need for people and many wake up to find that 'retirement' has struck some five or ten years prematurely, leaving an empty life stretching ahead.

If many of our friends and relatives sought a life elsewhere there are, equally, far more who see our climate, our land, our language and our way of life as more desirable than that of their own home-land, and Watford a desirable and thriving place in which to settle and serve. Over recent decades we have welcomed Caribbeans and Jamaicans who were invited by the Government of the day to come and work here (much as did the Australian Government when it attracted many from the UK). The immigrants found our winter climate hard to bear after their own warmth but most persevered; they spoke and understood English and soon integrated.

The ties with our 'Empire' were dissolved soon after WWII, but habit died hard and many of the colonies chose to remain connected as part of the British Commonwealth. Before, and after, WWII many from, for example, India chose to send their children to England for education, mainly in pro-fessions. Many chose to stay and second and third generations have been been born who are 'Indian' but have never seen India. Partition of India in 1947 resulted in strife between the new India and the new Pakistan and since 1960 a great number of immigrants have settled from Pakistan. Without the 'reverse colonial' practice of seeking higher education here many have settled with a rudimentary command of English with which to start and many are, like our own 1960s emigrants, artisans seek-ing a better life than that which they left. Troubles in parts of Africa meant that many of Indian ori-gin, who had settled and built businesses there, were forced out. They were welcomed here for their business acumen and industrious nature as were many 'settlers' of Irish and Italian extraction.

Today's unknown factor is whether our modern 'asylum seekers' will so well integrate

It is a far cry from the flint workers of 12,000 years ago; with a wide mix of racial origins, modern integration within Watford's communities has been peaceful and to everyone's benefit.

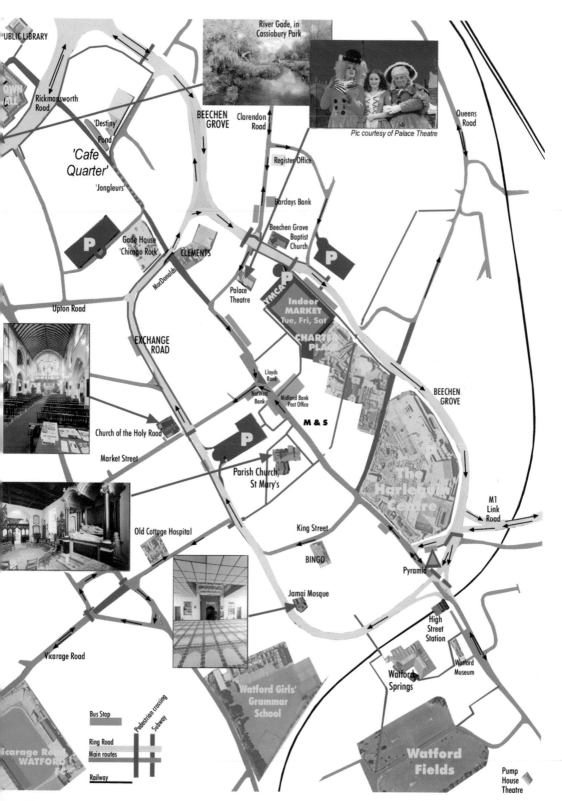

UBLIC LIBRARY

Rickmansworth Road

BEECHEN GROVE

Clarendon Road

River Gade, in Cassiobury Park

Queens Road

'Destiny' Pond

'Cafe Quarter'

'Jongleurs'

Register Office

Pic courtesy of Palace Theatre

Barclays Bank

Gade House 'Chicago Rock'

CLEMENTS

MacDonalds

Beechen Grove Baptist Church

Upton Road

EXCHANGE ROAD

Palace Theatre

YMCA

Indoor MARKET Tue, Fri, Sat

CHARTER PLACE

BEECHEN GROVE

Lloyds Bank

NatWest Bank

Midland Bank Post Office

M & S

Church of the Holy Rood

Market Street

Parish Church, St Mary's

The Harlequin Centre

M1 Link Road

Old Cottage Hospital

King Street

BINGO

Pyramid

Jamai Mosque

High Street Station

Vicarage Road

Watford Springs

Watford Museum

Bus Stop

Pedestrian crossing

Subway

Watford Girls' Grammar School

Ring Road

Main routes

icarage Road WATFORD FC

Railway

Watford Fields

Pump House Theatre

The road layout of the modern town centre. The ring road, except where marked, is not suitable for pedestrians. Watford Springs is no more and Clements is T J Hughes.

We started with the ford, and have travelled the dusty and muddy road into modernity; from the old houses turned into shops, in turn to replaced with modern stores to match the various ages, to the new pyramid age.

This, 1996, right, is built on the corner of the old Water Lane High/ High Street corner—shown a half-century ago on page 82 and just over a century ago on page 24; a vibrant shopping scene on page 91.

At the bottom the fields of Cassiobridge have seen the coming of Mr Jone's Print Works/Menpes Press/ Sun Engraving and Printers, lastly Odhams-Sun and now turned by machinery back to nature ready for building housing.

The mosaic sign 'Sun Engraving Company Ltd' over the entrance was photographed just before demolition.

Back in 1989 the gasworks area near the river Colne was cleared and looking towards the railway embankment this is the vista which appeared briefly. It is within a few yards of the site of Watford's Ford of historic ancestry.

2001/2 the 'Sun' was pulled down; the rubble crushed and the site levelled. This is 2003 awaiting the pile-drivers and builders . . .